THE HELPING PROCESS: AN INTRODUCTION

THE HELPING PROCESS:
An Introduction

DOUG MACLEAN AND SUE GOULD

CROOM HELM
London • New York • Sydney

© 1988 D. MacLean and S. Gould
Croom Helm Ltd, Provident House, Burrell Row,
Beckenham, Kent, BR3 1AT

Croom Helm Australia, 44-50 Waterloo Road,
North Ryde, 2113, New South Wales

Published in the USA by
Croom Helm
in association with Methuen, Inc.
29 West 35th Street
New York, NY 10001

British Library Cataloguing in Publication Data

MacLean, Doug
   The helping process : an introduction.
   1. Counseling
   I. Title II. Gould, Sue
   361.3'23   BF637.C6

   ISBN 0-7099-4682-1

Library of Congress Cataloging-in-Publication Data

MacLean, Doug.
   The helping process.

   Bibliography: p.
   Includes index.
   1. Counseling. 2. Helping behavior. I. Gould, Sue.
II. Title.
BF637.C6M26 1987   158'.3   87-24519
ISBN 0-7099-4682-1

Printed and bound in Great Britain by
Biddles Ltd, Guildford and King's Lynn

CONTENTS

Contents

Contents

LIST OF FIGURES

PREFACE

Over the past twenty years, there has been a proliferation of both popular and academic literature about counselling, helping techniques, communication strategies, analyses of human interaction, skills training, and the like. This has accompanied an expansion of the helping professions, of tertiary training courses for people wishing to enter the welfare field in one form or another, and of further and refresher education for professional helpers. What contribution, then, does a book such as this one have to offer?

One fundamental aspect of this book is its reaffirmation of some of the very basic, but so often overlooked or underplayed, principles of professional helping. The use of the word 'professional' here is advised - we do not refer just to helping activities undertaken by people who are trained and paid to do so, but more widely - to helping activities which are 'professional' in the sense that they are purposeful, informed and self-conscious. For those whose career in the helping area is embryonic, this book emphasises the importance of the establishment and maintenance of a working relationship with the client which is 'for better rather than for worse' for the client, and offers a variety of frames of reference, models, techniques and understanding of the skills required. The basis of such models and frames of reference is firmly grounded in social science theory and knowledge of human development - a requirement also stressed as essential to the development of skilled professional helping.

For those whose career in helping is more advanced, and who have the benefit of some practice wisdom, what this book may offer is a return to some critically important skills, theory and techniques, and some reframing of the helping enterprise in such a way as to cast new, different light upon established practice.

A great deal of the content in the chapters that follow has been used as the basis for a number of introductory courses in helping skills and the helping process. This text is a much expanded, and we hope, improved and updated version of an earlier set of notes on counselling produced by one of the authors (MacLean, 1980a). We have also developed a set of course notes for tutors, which include a series of exercises for students, some of which are for completion by individuals and some for group completion. Our courses tend to be highly participative in nature, following the text herein chronologically over approximately one academic term. Course tutors are invited to contact the authors direct if they are interested in obtaining information about this material which can be used in close conjunction with this book.

It is to be hoped that the message of this book about self-conscious helping, and about helping as an intervention for change, is as compelling as it is fundamental, we believe, to effective and professional helping.

Doug MacLean
Sue Gould

CHAPTER ONE

The Nature of Helping

1.1   What Is Helping?

Michael O'Brien, you wilfully broke and entered the Moana Yacht Club. You defecated on the Board-Room table; you wilfully destroyed furniture and fittings valued at over $50,000 and you forcibly entered the liquor storeroom smashing and destroying stocks of wine and spirits. There you drank yourself into a state of insensibility before being found by the security guard.

You are a danger to yourself, your family and to society as a whole. Notwithstanding that this is your first major offence and the nature of your personal circumstances - you are sentenced to two years Borstal training.

The Judge motioned dismissal with his hand, and Mike - eighteen years of age, a fresh-faced, tall, well-built young man - was ushered staggering from the dock by two police officers. His family watched in horror as he disappeared from sight.

*   *   *   *   *   *   *

This is not fiction! Mike served his two years training and upon release returned to his family. The 'personal circumstances' referred to by the Judge will be examined in some detail as a vehicle for beginning to understand and explore some of the issues surrounding the notion of helping.

But, what is helping? What does it mean to be helpful? These appear to be strange questions, because surely everyone knows what is meant by being helpful. Obviously, if someone appears to be in distress, then it seems perfectly natural to provide help or to offer assistance, comfort or solace. However, conjure up now a vision of another young man

1

purposefully, almost aggressively taking an old lady by the arm and steering her across a busy road, despite her protestations that she does not want to go that way. Our young hero doing his good deed, is in fact not being helpful at all. Perhaps he misreads the needs of the old lady, or perhaps he is pursuing his own need to do a good turn. Whatever the case, it is clear that a great number of ostensibly helpful acts are not really very helpful, at least for the unfortunate recipient. And, in the counselling situation, help in the form of counselling may not be to the client's advantage if, for example, it perpetuates a dependency relationship between worker and client.

In other words, there are dimensions to the helping process which may escape notice by a too superficial acceptance of the notion of helping. There is greater complexity inherent in the notion of what might be termed 'real helping' than offering solace to the bereaved; the handing out of anti-depressants to the depressed; a tranquiliser to the anxious; or merely listening to a call for help over the telephone. To be sure, these activities may be helpful, but it is also possible that in some instances activities intended to help may be quite destructive, leaving the recipient of help in a worse position than before the help was sought. Was this the situation with Mike and his family? The following are extracts from the social worker's case notes compiled after the first five sessions with Mike and his family.

Mike and his family:
Mike is 18; he is fifth in a family of six children. Other children in the family are Mary (31); Brian (29); John (26); Alice (27); and Julie (10). His sister Alice left home when Mike was 9, John left home a year earlier.

His mother describes Mike as a more or less model child. There were no problems at birth or in his early years, apart from the usual childhood illnesses. She admits that Mike was 'spoiled rotten' by the older children. Mike's father is a somewhat shadowy figure, being less than fit because of war injuries. He is a hardworking tradesman; taciturn in nature. Mother, on the other hand, is extremely dominant and in some ways overpowering in her desire to do the best for her children, all of them.

Mike is said to have welcomed the birth of Julie, and was, according to Mrs O'Brien, 'madly in love with her' all his life. 'He would do anything for her' and this included taking her for long walks, sometimes 5-8 kms when she was little. He would indulge her as much as possible. Occasionally there were one or two accidents but these, according to his mother, were not too serious. For example, when Mike somehow let go of Julie's pram on a hill. It was only the prompt action of a stranger which stopped it from crossing a busy road. Mike evidently slipped, or the

2

handbrake was not working too well.

Mike had the usual friends when at school according to his mother. He was of average ability but his school performance in all subject areas was significantly lower than his potential. He left school as soon as he was legally allowed to (aged 15). Mike said that he did not like school. He did not participate much in the life of the school or in any of its extra-curricula activities. He used to 'hang about' with a group of boys who, whilst not delinquent in any way, were always on the periphery of trouble.

Mike and his friends used to go out with a group of girls. There is no doubt that they were all sexually active. In fact, one of the girls, Judith, became pregnant. Mike's mother was sure that it was one of the other boys, and not Mike, that had got Judith pregnant. But, as her son had admitted sleeping with Judith, and all the other boys denied paternity, 'we made sure that he did his duty'. Mike was aged 16 when he married Judith. She was 15. He said that 'he had to do his duty by her'. Whilst acknowledging paternity of the child, Annie, it is not clear whether he is in fact the father. Mike and Judith's second child was born last year and is now about ten months old.

Not too much is known about Judith's background, but it is known that Judith comes from a small closely knit 'religious' family. She is the eldest of three children. Physically she is tall and willowy, looking somewhat anaemic, wan and tired. Whilst Mike's parents have been supportive, Judith's parents have more or less disowned her since the time of her first pregnancy and marriage.

Mike has been unemployed on and off since leaving school; this in a period of relatively little unemployment. He is a poor manager of money, and when 'flush' tends to drink to excess, and can become violent towards his wife. Mike's job performance is quite good when he is sober. After a few drinks, however, he tends to become angry with people and can become quite rude to customers and bosses alike. This tends to ensure that his stay in jobs is not for long.

He left his last job as a forecourt attendant at a petrol pump outlet and helped himself to some of the money from the till. He called it wages. Mike said that he took the money as they were so much in debt; he had to do something to relieve the pressure of creditors. His rent with the housing authority is in arrears. They owe, in addition, the equivalent of three months wages (before tax) to various other creditors throughout the community. He has been known to steal money from milk bottles.

Mike came under the notice of the welfare department as a result of the

3

theft from the petrol station. After discussions between the welfare department and the police, it was decided that no charges were to be laid by the police. This was conditional, however, upon Mike and his family agreeing to be placed under the 'preventative supervision' of the welfare department. The welfare department was then in a position to offer help to Mike and his family. If after being placed under 'preventative supervision', Mike and his family then refused to co-operate with the department, the department would have no option but to bow out of the situation.

The family is also in receipt of supplementary, hardship grants. These are additional to Mike's unemployment benefit, the receipt of which tends to be sporadic, because of the 'voluntariness' of Mike's unemployment. This means, for example, that each time Mike terminates his employment, he is placed on a standown period of 6 weeks, during which time, of course, he is not entitled to any benefit.

Their house is a tidy, three bedroom, government-subsidised place. It is barely furnished, and well kept as far as is possible by Judith, recognising the fact that she has two small children. Mike is good with the kids and loves his wife and the children dearly. He said that he would do almost anything for them. Judith reciprocates and has at no stage thought about getting out of the marriage.

* * * * * * *

Helping, then, involves intervening in the lives of others. It could be argued that even the offer of help is, in and of itself, an intervention. At a superficial level, at least, the notion of helping implies that the outcome of the helping ought to be of benefit to the helped. Yet, research seems to indicate that the contrary may be the case in many instances, and that 'helping may be for better or worse', (eg. Carkhuff and Berenson, 1967).

1.2 Questions For Helpers

There are a number of questions which helpers ought to think about and ponder upon in relation to their own helping. What really is the essence of helping? What happens when you help somebody? What do you do to them? What do you do for them? What do they do for you? What are you doing to, and for, yourself when you offer to help people? Are all your attempts at being helpful successful? How do you know whether or not you are a successful helper?

Let us consider some of these questions and issues in relation to Mike and his family. For example, if you had been the helper - the social worker -

at the time of Mike's first offence when he stole money from the petrol pump outlet, how do you think you would have gone about helping him? What might constitute 'help' to Mike at this time? Some people may argue, for instance, that help for Mike may be finding him another job, and perhaps, offering budget-counselling. Others may believe that Mike would be best helped by some 'deeper' therapeutic counselling approach exploring with him the methods of coping he has developed over time. Both of these approaches cited, are examples of differing forms of helping. It may be desirable to use more than one approach to helping, or to combine differing approaches. Crucial questions here include: How does a helper identify what might be the nature of the help required for any particular individual in need? How do you identify what form the help offered should take?

Associated with this is the question of your expectations as a helper. Consider Mike's progress as a client: he progressed from petty theft which brought him to the attention of the welfare system, to a more serious offence which culminated in his being sentenced to Borstal training. What do you think would have happened to you as the helper during the course of your contact with Mike? It is not uncommon for helpers to feel disillusioned, inadequate and frustrated when their efforts seem to have a dubious impact upon the continuing distress of a client. In Mike's case, for example, it is possible that the 'help' he received simply delayed his eventual demise in court - we will never know. Perhaps, the shock of being confronted with a severe reaction to his behaviour by the court - society - would have more of an impact on Mike's behaviour patterns than any other form of 'help'. If this is the case, then it could be argued, ironically, that efforts by a helper to prevent that confrontation are not, in fact, helpful to Mike in the long term! Whether or not the rest of society, including Mike's immediate family, would agree with this is another, equally valid matter, which helpers ought to consider. Helping Mike involves, among other things, a consideration of the nature of Mike's relating in a reasonable and satisfactory way to his social environment, as well as his attempting personal resolutions for his internal conflicts which may be at the root of his disruptive behaviour.

And what of Mike? What happened to him while he was being helped? Whatever else was going on, the sequence of events did not seem to have the effect of stabilising or enriching his life, or that of his family. Mike's behaviour became increasingly anti-social and destructive during that time. If we look at the information available in the case study material, does Mike appear to have the personal and social resources that he could utilise in changing his behaviour, or has Mike's fortune been well and truly told? Is his more seriously offensive behaviour a reflection of

5

frustration with the help he was receiving, or would this have happened anyway? Assessing the effectiveness of the intervention which is intended to be helpful is always difficult. How do you know when you have been helpful? Is it reasonable to make the assumption that help offered, especially professional help, will be of benefit to the recipient? Examining an assumption such as this is as crucial a part of the helping process as is the contact relationship with the client.

Mike's case highlights an important issue in the business of helping. The intention to help another is a necessary condition for helping. It is, however, by no means sufficient in and of itself, nor is its presence any guarantee of 'successful' helping. That is, although a high value is placed on the intention of helping, and perhaps upon a commitment to helping, this value position is intrinsically not enough. For associated with this value are beliefs about, for example, what the well-being of people entails, as well as knowledge about how and why people behave in the ways that they do, and what kinds of actions are required for change. This change may be to individuals and/or to the social context of which they are a part. Hence, helping is intimately tied up with values, beliefs and, knowledge about human beings, their nature (including their strengths, weaknesses, ways of relating to others and society, etc) and the kinds of skills and knowledge required to bring about change.

There are many situations in which we may find ourselves faced with a person in need of help, either in everyday living, or in our jobs as helpers, if that is the case. The kinds of questions for helpers which have been raised here are not of mere academic interest, nor are they purely exercises in semantics. They are crucial questions which are at the very heart of helping, and which have implications for those who want to be called helpers. Some of these implications, as we have seen, have to do with assumptions about what is helpful behaviour, values and beliefs about helping and about people's well-being, and so on. Consider some further examples of situations demanding intervention.

Mr Smith lived for some while in a block of twelve flats. He knew that next door to his left lived a couple of young women, aged in their early twenties; to his right, a person who worked at the University. Mr Smith spoke occasionally to both, but he knew nobody else in the block. Upon returning home one night, he heard one of the girls next door screaming, obviously in pain and very much afraid. She was, it transpired later, being beaten up by her latest boyfriend, who was shouting 'I need you, you bitch!' What would you do, in a situation such as this?

Imagine a main street or road in your neighbourhood, full of people. Your interest is aroused because of all the milling around; the noise and so on.

You push your way to the front of the crowd; there, you discover a police
constable lying on the ground, being kicked and jumped upon by a number
of men. Would you intervene, hoping to help in that situation? Would you,
perhaps, like the rest of the crowd continue to mill around waiting for
somebody else to assist the police officer? Or would you sneak away,
saying to yourself 'it's no business of mine, he must have asked for it!' A
few years ago a Salvation Army officer intervened in such a situation. He
was beaten-up very severely by the gang, who turned on him, after
accounting for the policeman. As a result of his injuries, he went into a
coma, and eventually died three years later, never having recovered
consciousness. The police officer returned to his duties after spending
some time in hospital. Stories abound of women being raped in broad
daylight in the major cities of the USA with nobody bothering to assist
the victim. Is it helpful to attempt to intervene as the Salvation Army
officer did? Is it helpful to ignore the situation?

There is a need for systematic and self-conscious helping - helping based
on clearly defined beliefs and values, and directed by well-researched
knowledge and self-conscious skills. This statement represents a point of
view, a philosophy about what we consider to be desirable elements in the
helping process, and which will be repeatedly expressed in this book.

Therefore, we will want to be consistent in uncovering and challenging
the values, beliefs and assumptions which underlie and direct our
behaviour as helpers. These values, beliefs and assumptions flow
inevitably into our helping behaviour - they affect the kinds of
judgements that we make about 'what is wrong with the client'; they
affect the nature of the resources available to the individual; they
influence the kind of help or intervention to be offered, presuming some
embryonic awareness of what the outcomes of our intervention might look
like. There will, then, be a great emphasis on the need for helpers to be
'self-aware'. This awareness must extend to the kinds of knowledge, skills
and methods available and pertinent to helping encounters in general,
and to particular cases. Going even further, it is important to be aware
of the knowledge, skills and methods that you are not using in a
particular case!

If, for example, you took the view that Mike was irresponsible, or that he
was unable to shoulder responsibility, what kinds of knowledge may
support your view? What might be the most appropriate forms of
intervention in assisting him to accept his responsibilities? What
objectives, short and long term, do you think would be desirable and
feasible? Much of what we do as helpers depends on what we consider
helping to be, and on how we define 'helping'.

7

What are the conditions under which intervention can be helpful? Are certain kinds of intervention better than others? Hindsight, for example, would suggest that had the Salvation Army officer acted more prudently, perhaps by calling for further assistance, he might be alive today.

1.3 Some Definitions of Helping

Loughary and Ripley (1979) suggest that 'Helping is providing purposeful assistance to other people which makes their lives more pleasant, easier, less frustrating, or in some other way more satisfying'.

In a more complex definition, Fischer (1973) believes that:

> ... interpersonal helping can be described as informed, purposeful intervention either directly with, or on behalf of, a given person or persons (client). The goal of such intervention is to bring about positive changes either directly in the client's functioning, or in environmental factors immediately impinging on the client's functioning. These interventions are intended to enhance aspects of the client's feelings, attitudes and/or behaviours in such a way that his personal and social functioning will be more satisfying and beneficial to him. (Fischer, 1973)

The Fischer (1973) definition goes further than that of Loughary and Ripley (1979) in that it suggests that helping is an 'interpersonal' process - that is, that it involves at least two parties - the helper and the person being helped - the client. It is important to note that the client may be an individual, group, family, organisation, community or nation-state. Both definitions point to the goals and purposes of the helping. Fischer suggests that the purpose of the helping is to make life 'more satisfying and beneficial to him' - that is, to the client. This is echoed by Loughary and Ripley.

But, who determines what is beneficial for the client? Who determines what is likely to be more satisfying to the client? Implicit in both these definitions is the suggestion that the client has a role to play in determining what the nature of the outcome ought to be, unlike the old lady being forced across the road, or Mike being sentenced to Borstal. Mike did have a role in the helping process, but apparently this made little difference. Note, however, that Fischer's definition does not necessarily include the idea of 'fitting' the client into his society, but it is concerned with the client's attitudes, behaviours and feelings so that he can better live with himself and in his interpersonal relating.

Both these definitions beg a number of very serious questions, however.

Are you entitled to intervene in any other person's life? Provided the results of your actions are 'positive' does it matter what methods or procedures you adopt to attain such goals? If, for example, a young adolescent girl is 'having trouble' with her parents, should you encourage her to leave home, or more drastically to shoot her parents, in order to solve the problem? In the case of Mike, would it have been legitimate for a worker to have counselled Judith to seek a divorce from Mike? Under what conditions are you as a helper 'entitled' to intervene, to help? This is not as far-fetched as it sounds. A number of helpers have so narrowed the focus of their helping to that of the 'presenting client' that they have ignored the environment, human and physical, in which their client lives, to the detriment of all concerned.

Helping, in both definitions, is seen as being 'purposeful' and 'informed' (Fischer, 1973). This suggests that not only is the helping behaviour purposeful in the sense of attempting to achieve some goal or objective of benefit to the client, but that it is purposeful in that it is intentional. The helper intends to assist the client. This, then, precludes from the ambit of helping those behaviours of the helper which fortuitously assist the client. Helping, according to Fischer must be informed - that is, informed by a knowledge of human behaviour, growth, development, and personality, as well as by a knowledge of what is involved in helping. Informed, in other words, by theory from a variety of sources and disciplines which impinge upon the human condition. Furthermore, implicit in the Fischer definition of helping is the suggestion that helping cannot merely be seen as the utilisation of a 'recipe-book' approach of a compendium of appropriate skills, without the understanding and knowledge that underlies those particular skills.

As has been mentioned previously, the twin notions of being 'informed' and 'purposeful' tend to rule out those activities which may be helpful, and which people use naturally. That is, these definitions point beyond mere chatting with and listening to neighbours and their trials and tribulations. Many trainee-helpers believe that the ability to be sociable is both necessary and sufficient for helping - this is not so. Though, of course, these qualities are helpful, if built upon by being informed and purposeful in the helping situation. Mere sociability is no substitute for helping.

Helping, to be effective, has to be a purposeful and informed activity which is primarily aimed at enabling the person being helped to help himself. Help has also been defined

> as providing conditions for people to fulfill their needs for
> security, love and respect, self-esteem, decisive action and

self-actualising growth. (Brammer and Shostrum, 1977.)

This latter definition adds the idea of the helper providing the climate, conditions, or environment for growth, the purpose of which is clearly to enable the person being helped to assist themselves. There is, in all this, the other idea that there ought to be a movement within the person towards autonomy or independence of action and separateness from the worker.

If you were Mike's social worker or helper what would you do that represents informed, purposeful intervention, and that in time might lead to his being a more autonomous individual? If you thought that part of Mike's difficulty was coping with responsibility, then you might turn to Glasser's Reality Therapy for inspiration (Glasser, 1965). If on the other hand, you believed that the nature of the mother-Mike relationship was problematical, then you may turn to a more 'dynamically' orientated approach (Bordin, 1968) as a means of understanding more about Mike and his current functioning. Other helpers may suggest that there are contingencies in the environment that are shaping Mike's behaviour, and if these can be discovered and the environment changed then there could well be a change in Mike's behaviour. Most theorists would not disagree with the fact that helping ought to be informed, purposeful intervention; their disagreement with each other would be in terms of what the goals and purposes of the intervention are, and the means to attain those goals. It may well be that the differences stem from differences in underlying philosophies and values.

1.4   The Basic Elements of the Helping Situation

The definitions of helping previously discussed imply that there are at least four elements to be considered in the helping situation. There is, first of all, the client who seeks assistance, or who by his very actions, may oblige others to force him to seek help. The client may be an individual, group, family, community or organisation. It is extremely important to be sure who in fact the client is! Failure to identify the 'real' client can be extremely destructive, time-wasting and ineffective for all concerned. A client has rights and obligations, and is 'protected' by statements within professional codes of ethics. Not an uncommon feature of many families in distress is the emergence of the 'victim' who may be frequently 'pushed' forward as the client. Concentrating on the victim of the family pathology may do nothing about the malaise within the family. In fact, the removal of the victim from the confines of the family, frequently results in the emergence of a new 'victim'. Clients may espouse similar values to your own; they may come from any ethnic group and from all walks of life. They may come for assistance for profound personality disturbances or merely for information from a Citizens

Advice Bureau (CAB).

The second element in the helping situation is the person of the helper. Helpers may be school counsellors, medical practitioners, ministers of religions, lawyers, CAB workers. They may be professionally trained with a degree or professional qualification in social work or counselling. Some are para-professionals working with a Government or local body agency, perhaps not formally qualified but with years of experience on the job, and whose training may be a combination of both attendance at 'block courses', sometimes of several weeks' duration, and training 'on the job'. Helpers may be 'lay people' seeking to assist others through working for voluntary social work or welfare agencies, religious or secular, usually in a part-time capacity.

The only tool that a helper has, is himself. Helpers usually cannot administer drugs or other medical-type treatments - 'the talking cure' requires the dynamic use of the self, and hence as mentioned earlier, the need for self-awareness on the part of the helper. Usually, helpers tend to be more mature, emotionally stable, and more open and flexible than those seeking help. If it were the other way around, then the worker might end up on the receiving end of counselling. The helper is a crucial ingredient in developing the third element within helping - the relationship.

The helping relationship is an intangible created through the interaction of the helper and the client. It is the relationship which is the vehicle for any change in the client. Someone once observed that all helping takes place within a relationship. It is almost impossible to conceive of helping taking place outside a relationship; even if that relationship is one between the individual and himself, or one between the individual and his God! The problem is, however, that having argued that all helping takes place within a relationship, it must be emphasised that not all relationships are helpful! Certainly, many so-called helping relationships between counsellors and their clients have been less than productive, and many quite destructive.

The fourth element to be touched on here, that exists in all helping, is the context or parameters within which both parties to the helping encounter have their existence. In one sense this encompasses the wider society and its institutions which have a part in structuring our lives. At a more intimate level, it is a recognition that clients (and helpers) live, grow, and work, and have their being legitimated in small primary groups like the family. When you encounter a client in your work, you are encountering a person with a history and who exists within a context which you may need to understand before you can work effectively. In the case of Mike, he had a dominant mother, was the only child for a number of years, and was spoiled by his older siblings. He reacted deeply to the birth and subsequent development of his sister. His Mother was so dominant in his life that she defined for Mike a course of action that was to direct his life for years - he must do his duty by his wife! Mike's history and his connectedness with his family are, surely, keys in the understanding of this unfortunate young man.

The four elements within the notion of helping will be explored in more detail in later chapters within this book. So far we have outlined some of the assumptions which we believe underpin notions of helping. Some of these include a belief in the essential ability of clients to take hold of their own lives, to make decisions and to own their behaviour. One goal in helping is to move the client towards greater autonomy and control over his own life. Helping has to be an intentional act of intervention in the lives of others, which is purposeful and informed. The very act of intervention causes us to be sensitive to the rights of clients not to be 'intervened upon'. This sensitivity raises a number of issues which, we, as counsellors constantly confront, and which direct us to the consistent requirement to evaluate our work, re-examine our values and re-appraise our degree of self-awareness and competence.

CHAPTER TWO

The Helping Process

2.1 Overview

The previous chapter defined what is meant by helping and outlined four of the basic elements involved in helping. These were:

1. the helper;
2. the client;
3. the relationship that is created between them; and
4. the context or environment within which the helping takes place.

This chapter continues this discussion of helping by focusing, inter alia, on some of the steps we believe are inherent within the helping process.

Helping can be regarded as the process which begins with a client seeking assistance from the helper to resolve some difficulty which she is experiencing. The helper at the request of the client then intervenes in some purposeful way which, hopefully, results in a positive outcome for the client. Thus, the helping process can be broken into a number of steps or stages, and it will pay you to have the overview of the total helping process in mind as you work with clients.

This is not to say that each step or stage in the process has to be slavishly adhered to, nor does it mean that the sequence of stages is invariant. What it does mean, however, is that the encounter with your client in the here and now, with its overpowering and, at times overwhelming immediacy, has to be seen in a much larger context. There has to be the recognition that this particular interview is likely to be one of many, and there has to be cognisance of the fact that this interview is but one part of a larger, overall process taken over a number of interviews. Experience has shown that a number of helpers are very good at the beginning stages of helping, but very poor at the latter stages in the helping process. This is often because they have no overall idea of the management of the helping process.

2.2 Some Models of the Helping Process

Stages in the helping process can be identified in almost any contact with any client over any number of interviews. Broadly speaking, these stages fall into three main areas - problem clarification; assistance; problem resolution and termination of contact (Loughary & Ripley, 1979). These will be dealt with in sequence.

Firstly, the terms 'problem clarification', 'diagnosis', 'appraisal' and 'assessment' are analogous terms used by many writers to describe an activity that is essential in any helping process. That is, to put it rather crudely, to discover what it is that is bothering the client. What is going wrong and needs to be changed? Simple, and yet so complex.

Let us consider for a moment some of these terms in more detail. 'Problem clarification' as a process may not tell us what is bothering the client, but, it may assist the client in deciding what is wrong in his or her life situation. There is a difference! The difficulty with this is that the client may be reporting, for example, feelings of depression, or feelings of persecution. It may not be helpful to the client to further wallow in these feelings which may arise or be exacerbated in any attempt to clarify them. The expression of these feelings may well reflect the client's responses to the problem rather than being the problem.

The term 'diagnosis' has strong medical connotations, and for many in the helping area it is a term which suggests implicitly the medical model of illness. This may be inappropriate in the non-medical helping sphere, where notions of 'cure' do not always make too much sense, (for example can you really 'cure' delinquency, or the impact of a history of child-abuse?) Diagnosis does, however, point to inherent weaknesses within the client which may be experienced as a 'dis-ease': a degree of marked discomfort with herself and her relationship with her environment. The notion of diagnosis and the inherent medical model does recognise that there may well be something that is going awry and that this may require some kind of change.

Helping, as mentioned earlier, is an intervention; and the purpose of that intervention is to facilitate change within the client, her environment, or both. Problem clarification, as a term, lacks any very strong commitment to change, and so it should be seen as only a part of the initial helping stage. We believe that the notion of 'appraisal' has, however, built into it a more holistic view of the individual.

Appraisal suggests that the individual, the client, has to be seen as possessing strengths as well as weaknesses. The most appropriate way, therefore, of effecting change may be to enhance the possibilities latent within the client, and not to concentrate on her deficits. Furthermore, the notion of appraisal seems to us to go beyond the mere individual, insisting that the individual has to be seen as a whole person within an environment. The individual inhabits, or is part of, an ecological system. A factor frequently forgotten by helpers.

The term 'assessment' has a strong evaluative flavour, and suggests the use of tests and other instruments that measure client capacity or performance in a variety of areas of functioning. Assessment may assist in the discovery of what is wrong, and may in many instances precede the making of a 'diagnosis' or statement of what is believed to be the difficulty that the client is experiencing.

Whatever term you use to describe the initial stages of helping, it needs to be scrutinised carefully, and the assumptions and values underpinning it, exposed. The terms you use may be the consequences of your philosophy and values, and hence, not only have a role in influencing perceptions of clients and their problems, but also in structuring the nature of your work with them. Depending on the nature of the terms used, you will tend to ask different kinds of questions, and the map that you draw, on the basis of the information obtained, could well vary.

Secondly, after discovering what you think might be the problem, (and it may be important to distinguish the 'presenting' problem from the 'real' problem), some decision has to be made about what ought to be done. This second area of activity is concerned with the nature of the intervention - the assistance to be offered. We are concerned with what is to be done, who is to do it, and how it is to be achieved. This involves inevitably some idea of the goals or objectives of the contact. For example, if you believe that your client has poor self-esteem and that this is crippling her relationships with others in such a way that she is unable to find employment, then there is little point in offering her tranquilisers. To be sure, they may reduce her anxiety, but perhaps not much else. There has to be congruence between what you think the problem may be, the goals or objectives that might flow from this, and the methods by which you are to engage in helping to bring about a more desirable state of affairs for the client. If all goes well, then the problem is resolved.

Thirdly, we believe that as part of the problem resolution process, the helper must critically evaluate his work with the client in an objective way. In addition, the client's progress has to be evaluated. How has she done in relation to what was hoped for? Failure to achieve goals may be a function of a number of factors; these factors may include, for example, your work as a counsellor and helper; your client's intransigence; failure to take into account ecological pressures which mitigate against change; the setting of inappropriate goals and objectives, and so on.

There will always be failures. Some of our failures provide us with the possibility of great growth as helpers. Not that we should 'dynamically try to fail'! There is a host of reasons why helping can be for 'worse' rather than for better, and careful evaluation of the quality of helping is indeed a must. Evaluation of helping endeavours is a complex and reflective process. It must be ongoing, and we place high value on this vital activity by which helping can become more self-conscious and potentially more effective. The outcome of our work with a client should be an enhancement of the client's quality of life. It goes without saying that the outcomes should have been a consequence of our helping activity, and not merely a chance occurrence.

In all helping, then, it appears to us that there are these three fundamental areas of activity. The activity within each area may vary; Okun(1976), for example, divides the helping process into eleven steps encompassed within two overlapping stages:-

    (1) relationship
    (2) strategies.

There is a sense in which the above two can be called stages, and there is certainly some kind of sequence. Relationship building tends to be the focus of the initial encounters between helper and client, and once this is established the emphasis shifts towards the use of strategies. Both, obviously are operative within an interview, and over a number of interviews, but Okun is pointing to the predominant activity, the figure rather than the ground. The relationship has to be maintained during the strategies stage, and the very fact that you are in the relationship-building stage, implies the use of strategy.

The two stages, however, do not just overlap, they are inextricably intertwined. The use of the word 'stage' may be inappropriate. What we appear to have, may perhaps, be better thought of, as sets of focal activities, which may change during an interview, and certainly ought to change over the total contact with the client. It could well be argued that Okun has omitted to emphasise that as a relationship begins to terminate, there is a shift back from 'strategy' type activities to more of the relationship-building activity. The crucial difference being that the relationship-building at the beginning of an interview or work with the client is designed to create dependency, whereas the nature of the relationship-building towards the termination of contact, is towards independency and, autonomous behaviour on the part of the client.

In Okun's view, however, the relationship stage, comprising five steps, focuses on the importance of the development of a warm, trusting relationship between client and helper. It is this kind of relationship, Okun believes, that is a **sine qua non** for effective helping. Certainly, a number of disparate approaches to helping (eg. the so-called Client-Centered approach of Rogers, and Glasser's Reality Therapy) see this as an extremely important part of their approach. Other approaches do not put quite the same emphasis on the nature of the relationship (eg. Ellis' Rational Emotive Therapy, and the many behavioural approaches). Probably all approaches to helping, however, do depend upon some degree of co-operation by and with the client. To that extent, at least, the nature of the relationship that exists between client and helper is important.

The second stage - strategies - is concerned with the ways (the means, procedures, etc.) in which the relationship can be built upon to assist the client resolve her difficulties. There has to be a rationale behind the strategy being adopted and the possible implications for the client adopting a particular course of action (strategy) vis-a-vis others, explored.

Contact is terminated when the outcomes desired by the client are achieved. It is possible to use a number and a variety of strategies, capitalising on the work of the major theorists and practitioners. A helper may prefer, however, to operate within a particular frame of reference to the virtual exclusion of others. It is important that the strategy or strategies adopted by the helper should be the outcome of the conscious decision-making of the worker. Our experience has been that much poor quality helping is a function of the utilisation, by helpers, of ad hoc strategies, based on inarticulated theory (their own!) and as a result, they take actions which they find difficult to justify. We consider that this can be overcome to some extent, if the helper has a descriptive model of the kinds of activities in which he should be involved.

Stewart et al. (1978) use a 'systems' approach to helping, and they describe the helping process in an elegant flow-diagram. The process comprises twelve major stages, with most stages consisting of a number of smaller steps. The model has particular value as a prompt for what ought to be done next, and is, therefore, especially useful for certain jobs and conditions, such as school counsellors, and those workers who have heavy case-loads, where time is of the essence.

2.3 Flow-Diagram of the Helping Process
The flow-diagram (fig. 2.1) and ensuing discussion follow both the ideas of Okun (1976) and Stewart et al. (1978) modified to take into account

17

the four basic elements in helping, outlined in the previous chapter. The first three stages emphasise the preparatory activity of the helper prior to the client's coming in for help. In most cases, a client makes an appointment, giving an outline in brief of her problem. This gives an opportunity for the counsellor in a school situation, for example, to obtain and to review school records on the pupil. It may be that the data collected previously may be irrelevant to the matter that the client is bringing to the counsellor, but it pays to be prepared. We have been amazed, for example, at the number of counsellors in schools who have interviewed the wrong child, or have been responding to the client on the basis of the 'wrong' case notes.

In fact, you demonstrate that you care for your client when you are obviously prepared for her. You also demonstrate caring when you are on time for your interview with the client and show that you are prepared to give her the time she needs to 'tell her story, in her own way, at her own pace and in her own time.'

Step 1 in the model is entitled 'the helper'. The helper is accountable for his work, and so it is incumbent on helpers to be prepared 'within themselves' for the forthcoming interview. Any matter which is seriously troublesome to you, whether this is in your private life, or in your professional capacity as a worker, is likely to affect worker performance. It, therefore, behoves helpers in such situations to either postpone the interview, or have the client referred to another worker. If, for example, there is any leftover matter that exists in your relationship with your client, assuming that there is to be continuing contact, then that matter ought to be aired and worked upon under the supervision of another skilled worker, before you see your client. You have to be 'clear' before you can work with someone who may be quite distressed or emotionally disturbed. Failure to do so may add to the client's confusion, and you have no right to add to the burdens of a person already burdened! So there is a need to focus on yourself, before you move into the interview. This is extremely difficult, and those with heavy workloads in welfare departments or branches may argue that this is a luxury they cannot afford! We would, however, reiterate the necessity for making the time to focus in on yourself, as part of the process of self-awareness - a process which we believe is necessary for good, effective helping. Therefore, this time is a luxury you cannot not afford!

Step 4 in the model points to the need to explain to the client the nature of the helping which is offered by your agency in general and by you in particular. This stage is useful in describing the limits of the contact between the parties and the rights and obligations of each. It is also an important stage in that it assists in setting out the context within which

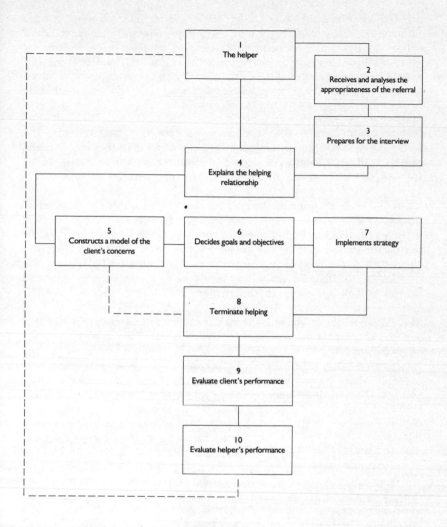

Figure 2.1: Flow — diagram of the helping process

the helping should take place. For example, if a client comes to you for information about obtaining a loan from a government agency, it is not within the limits of that helping relationship to discuss the client's (or your) sex life. There may appear to be a feeling of artificiality about this stage. In some agencies this is overcome by the drawing up of a formal contract between the parties. Some schools also use this as a technique of social control, and it works very well!

The argument here is that for many workers and their clients, the relationship is ambiguous, and with a great many disturbed clients, the provision of some degree of order, of comprehensibility of the world, through the judicial use of contract, may in itself be therapeutic.

Okun, in her description of the helping process calls this the 'initiation' or 'entry' stage. The worker or helper warmly welcomes the client and attempts to make her feel at ease. In the first three stages, the emphasis was on the preparation by the helper for the forthcoming interview. The focus in step four is on the development of a climate - the beginnings of a relationship - wherein the client feels secure and trusted - secure enough to tell her story to the helper.

The ability to obtain the story from the client is most important, for it is the 'story' information that provides the parameters within which you will have to work to construct a model of the client's concerns. If the relationship being built between helper and client is suspect, then it is probable that the information received from the client may also be suspect. Clients can be very selective about what they tell and to whom they tell, and this is particularly so when dealing with the parents of children who are in difficulty, and who maybe have contact with more than one agency. The one family may be on the books of more than one agency with ostensibly differing problems presented to the agencies, but in fact there might well be one underlying 'cause' or 'story'.

Step 5 in the model is concerned with the clarification and initial exploration of the client's difficulties, or the reasons she has sought your help. The clarification process may take time. Patience is needed because the problem which the client presents to you initially may in fact not be the real problem. To tease out any underlying problems, if they exist, and to have them accepted by the client as possibilities, takes great skill. It may well be that a professional judgement has to be made about whether or not it is appropriate to explore some of the more latent difficulties of which the client is, perhaps, only partially aware. This kind of confrontation with its heavy interpretative element needs careful handling.

Sometimes clients are so relieved to be able to talk about their problems that they will pour out their problems in a never-ending rush. It then becomes difficult to sort out not only the order in which problems should be tackled, but also which problems are the real problems. Some of the skills outlined in later chapters, are useful in this respect. Summarisation, for example, has a number of functions, one of which may be enabling the worker to get her breath back and to try and make sense of the outpourings from the client. At other times, clients will 'test' the helper out, perhaps with a superficial problem, or sometimes with an outburst to shock the helper.

At other times, the client will remain almost mute, as though deathly afraid to disclose her very real personal problems. In these cases all you can do is to offer to assist, and then wait for the client to tell her story at her own pace and time, in her particular way.

From the variety of problems outlined by the client, the helper has to decide which ones amongst them are amenable to the help offered by the agency, and then gain the agreement of the client that these particular problems should be examined. This leads to Step 6 which focuses on the joint decision of both helper and client about the goals or the objectives of the helping. In many cases of course, this is explicit in the initial request of the client: 'I would like a loan'; or it is obvious because of the particular function of your agency. You do not, for example, usually go to an abortion agency for careers material!

Mandala Mapping
A useful technique that can be used at this stage is called Mandala Mapping (see Fig. 2.2 for an example, using some of the material from the case study material on Mike, presented in Chapter One). Unlike the normal interview, which may be conducted across a desk, or sitting facing each other, use of the Mandala Map involves the worker and client working side by side, and together initially identifying the crucial areas, key persons, and significant events in the client's life.

The second phase of the Mandala Mapping process considers in turn, each one of the areas identified by the client in terms of their importance for the client, and whether or not there are difficulties being experienced in any particular area. This phase of the process involves obtaining the client's views and overall perceptions of each of the areas. Gentle probing by the helper, without judgement, can help the client to articulate and to clarify just what it is that she wants to say about each of the areas.

In the third phase the client decides which of all the areas identified,

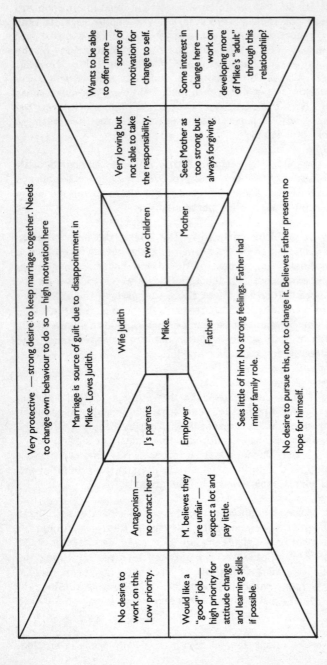

Note: "1" sectors = people/issues of significant concern to the client.

   "2" sectors = client's general view of those people/issues.

   "3" sectors = indication of client's desire to change or act on significant concerns.

   More sectors could be added. A fourth sector may be used to signify helper's actions and goals, for example.

Figure 2.2: An example of Mandala Mapping

(those areas with and those without problems or concerns), she would like to look at a little more closely. Having identified the areas to be considered, the next step is to ask what would the client like to happen in relation to that part or aspect of the client's life; what could be done and how does she think it could be achieved.

Then, from that point, decisions can be made about what is possible, together with the setting of goals or objectives and making a time for another interview at which time the client will report back, thus enabling the client to evaluate her own progress in relation to the goals and objectives set. The last phase, then, at some later date, involves an evaluation of the extent to which the client was able to realise her goals and objectives.

The critical aspects of Mandala Mapping are, firstly, that a dialogue is established between worker and client, and secondly, that the client is in control of the process. The client decides what areas in her life are first of all to be placed on the map; then what she will discuss in relation to each of them; the priority in which they will be discussed; what should be done and the means by which it will be achieved and how well she has done in relation to the goals that she set for herself.

If goals or objectives are stated, it becomes obvious that helping will cease when the goals or objectives have been reached. It may be that when that time comes, the decision is made to explore further problems and take additional action to resolve them. For example, a family who receives budgeting help, and who successfully clears their debt over a period of time, may seek additional help for their son's alcoholism. This is likely to happen if the relationship established between the worker and the family is a sound one.

Steps 5, 6, 7, 8 in the flow-diagram of the helping process may provide a loop, which allows for the modification of goals and objectives once the initial objectives have been achieved. The possibility of the existence of the loop also means that workers can assist with what may appear to be fairly superficial problems or difficulties, and that once 'trust' has been developed then the focus can shift away from the superficial to some of the more deeply personal problems the client may be experiencing. Typical of this pattern is the school child who goes to the counsellor for help with career planning. If this is handled well by the counsellor, there is a possibility that the child will 'front-up' with what really is the problem. There is a sense in which the client needs contact with the helper, in order to decide whether or not to 'self disclose'. This kind of 'testing' by clients is quite usual. The existence of the loop suggests that there is always the possibility of other difficulties being disclosed by the client. Of course, the worker can use the existence of the loop, to suggest to her client that whilst she came to discuss xyz, perhaps the real thing that ought to be discussed is abc. In that way, the contract between helper and client can be constantly modified, and helper exploration of client's concerns legitimated.

Helping is terminated when the client believes that some resolution of her problem has been attained. The model indicates that the client's performance has to be evaluated. This is a mutual process between helper and client and the client is free, as she is at any time, to terminate contact with the helper. Termination may also be suggested by the helper, particularly if a referral to some other agency is in prospect. The final step in the helping process is an evaluation of the helper's performance. In this stage, the helper, usually in consultation with a colleague or supervisor, closely examines the activity of the helper in working with the client. The particular focus of this evaluation should be on the helper's ability to create the climate and relationship in which the client can begin to discuss and explore her problems, and the utilisation of strategies which enable the client to resolve them.

A model of this kind, offers the helper an overview of the helping process. It suggests some of the stages that are important in this process. It provides a means of structuring helper activity: an important ingredient implicit in the notion that helping is 'purposeful and informed' intervention in the life of the client.

2.4   Values and Assumptions Underlying the Helping Process
The flow-diagram of the helping process presents, in a non-theoretical way, an overall description of the stages and the manner in which they may be linked to give the idea of movement through the process from initial contact to termination.

But what of the values and assumptions which underlie the helping process itself, and which we believe are present at every step of the way? We have previously stated the importance of articulating the values and assumptions which direct our helping activity as a part of our belief in self-conscious, informed, and purposeful helping. What are some of the assumptions? What, for example, is implied and may be perhaps hidden in the following simple description of one person helping another?

Mary helps John towards attaining X (where X is the end result of the help) for the benefit of John.

This activity - one person helping another - is not pursued indiscriminately. For example, if Mary is a law abiding citizen, she is unlikely to help John to rob a bank. That is, Mary will help John to the extent that in so doing, she does not excessively contravene her own beliefs and values. Value-free helping is a myth; our initial statement about helping requires, therefore, some elaboration. The statement about Mary and John can be broken into a number of discrete elements:

(1) Mary helps John;
(2) to X;
(3) for John/others;
(4) in $.

If we take each element of this statement in turn, some of the hidden or implicit themes present in even the simplest of one-to-one helping encounters are highlighted.

Element (1) - 'Mary helps John' - implies a one-way process. But is this necessarily so? Does Mary not benefit at all by her identifying John as the client? Indeed she does! Riessman (1965), for example has suggested that through the operation of the 'Helper Therapy Principle' there is clear evidence that Mary does indeed benefit. In fact, in self-help groups such as Synanon, and Alcoholics Anonymous, it is the leaders as helpers whose commitment to change in themselves is most strongly confirmed. Similarly, Volkman and Cressey (1963) have argued from research into the rehabilitation of criminals that when those who have been the clients have a chance to become helpers, they experience the helper role as more helpful to themselves than was their experience of the client role. Hence, that Mary benefits from the helping is fairly likely. What we should be especially concerned about is the extent to which John can and does benefit from a situation most probably helpful to Mary.

This does not deny the validity of the assistance offered by Mary, nor does it suggest that the nature of the 'help' Mary receives is similar to that of the client - John. Very little of the help offered is ever truly altruistic, and recognition of the fact that we, as helpers, are beneficiaries in the encounter, argues for continuous appraisal of our work. Where the benefits are greater for the worker than for the client, it may be that the helping is for the worse - for the client. It is legitimate for helpers to feel pleased about their work if successful (however that is defined). It is another matter, however, to use the encounter with your client to show how clever you are, or to inappropriately self-disclose, or to pursue some line of discussion which gives you a 'kick' or gives you the opportunity for an 'ego-trip'!

So, if for example, Mary helps John in order to meet her needs, she may be more likely to behave in such a way as to encourage John's dependence upon her, since it is the maintenance of the relationship which is of value to her. If Mary were in private practice, the continued maintenance of John's dependence upon her certainly affects her income!

In order for Mary to help John, there is an assumption that John was come to Mary (or her agency) for help. John could have been 'obliged' to seek help because of what was happening within him, or in his relationship to his environment. His state of 'dis-ease', of 'un-wellness', pushed or motivated him to obtain help. This is, in a sense, a weak version of obligation. In a stronger version, agents of social control, whether this be within his immediate network, (for example, family, relatives or colleagues), or the result of the efforts of officials (doctors, the courts, schools, etc.) have some role in John's being in contact with the helper. In the latter case, John may protest that he does not need help at all. Mary's response to John in each of these situations may well vary, and in turn may determine whether or not John perceives Mary as a helpful person.

The second element within the statement: 'to X', is an acknowledgement of the dynamic quality of the relationship between John and Mary. It is a relationship predicated on the notions of purpose and change. The purpose of the encounter is to enable John to obtain some goal or objective; to achieve that may mean a change in John, in Mary, in John's environment or all of these! In the flow-diagram, the outcome of Mary's constructing a model of John's concerns, is the setting of goals and/or objectives. The specification of these would suggest that the direction and target of change is known to both parties. However, in much helping, the assumption that both John and Mary perceive the same direction and target may be an invalid one, unfortunately. This assumption is challenged when we consider a number of possible variations on the theme of directions and targets.

The first variation we have called **compliance.** Consider a situation in which, while both parties overtly agree with each other as to what the concerns and goals are, they privately disagree. The 'model prisoner' may be a case in point. The prisoner behaves in order to secure early release; the prison officer believes that the good behaviour is a result of personal change, and thus recommends early release for the prisoner. The participants in such a situation would each intend to change the other in some way, while explicitly behaving as though their perspective of 'X' coincided. Note that the prison officer, however, always has the edge - he has overt external 'control' because of his ability to punish and frustrate the attainment of the goal by the prisoner. The prisoner then complies in order to obtain 'X'. The problem for the prison officer will be the doubt in his own mind as to whether or not the changes in the prisoner are 'real'.

The second variation we have called **co-operation**. That is: John and Mary openly and privately agree upon what the nature of 'X' should be and decide to co-operate in working to that end. Like the prisoner-officer situation above, the goals would be the same; the behaviour of the prisoner may also appear to be the same at least superficially. But, in the first situation the discerning eye may detect an element of 'toadying': of over-weaning compliance. On the other hand, in this second, co-operative relationship, real change - change that has been internalised - would be manifested in behaviour that would appear to be more genuine and authentic. However, John's recidivism may be the only way in which it might be possible to distinguish whether or not the change has occurred through compliance rather than through co-operation.

If Mary and John manifestly disagree about the nature of the helping and the goals and purposes of the helping, then, there exists a state of **competition**, - the third variation on the theme - between the two parties. In a prisoner-officer situation, this may result in the waging of guerilla warfare; trying, for example to set up the other party, and get them into trouble. In this situation, the prisoner in no way legitimates the officer's right to help. It is also likely, moreover, that the offer of help from the officer or Mary, as the case may be, is an attempt to satisfy individual needs.

A fourth logical possibility in this analysis, is that John and Mary disagree openly about 'X' but privately agree. The prisoner in our example, has two audiences in mind. He reacts negatively in an open manner to satisfy, perhaps, peer-group pressure for non-compliance. Internally, however, he is trying to make changes. There is **collusion** between the parties! This may occur in settings where clients do not refer themselves for help, but are instead referred and compelled to engage in such contact.

Further, an underlying assumption here is that not only is it possible to conceive of goal 'X' at all, (ie. it is possible to foresee the results of help), but also that some criterion for having attained 'X' is known. Again, John and Mary may differ as to their perception of whether or not 'X' has been attained. For every action we take, there are what are called manifest and latent functions. The manifest functions are those outcomes which are obvious and overt, and which have been previously defined as being appropriate. The latent functions are those consequences which flow from our actions, although they were not considered, or taken into account, initially. For example, the 'bureaucratic-political' decision to decentralise Government Employment Offices had the manifest function of making it easier for the unemployed to register in their local area. It also had the effect of reducing the unemployment or 'dole queues' - thus, making it difficult for many to believe that there was an unemployment problem at all! This latter, unintended effect, is an example of a latent function. In other words, as was mentioned in Chapter One, any offer of help is an intervention, and as such there may well be latent consequences of such an offer as well as from the help given.

The third element in the statement - 'for John/others' - raises the question of who is supposed to be the beneficiary of the help. It has been noted that the intended beneficiary of help is John, but that John's role as client probably benefits Mary and others as well as, or instead of, him. For example, it may be to a mother's advantage to have her son deemed a delinquent, particularly, if this means that the focus of blame is shifted onto his shoulders and he is removed from home, thus giving her a greater degree of freedom.

Because 'helping' has notions of 'goodness' built into it, it is assumed that the outcome of helping is in some way more desirable than no helping! There is no unequivocal way of testing this assumption and nor is there any guarantee that the giving of help means that the client is receiving benefit. Hence if John does not experience benefit as an outcome of help at any given time, then help has not, by John's definition taken place, notwithstanding the beliefs that Mary may hold about having helped him.

Therefore, in any evaluation of the helping process, the perceptions of both John and Mary have to be taken into account. This raises a number of issues which will be lightly touched upon here. First of all, as self-awareness is always partial, it may well be that John has obtained some benefit from his contact with Mary, in ways that are not within John's awareness. To suggest that no helping has taken place, may be just as erroneous as suggesting that helping has occurred.

Secondly, benefit may be a function of the future. Frequently, both in helping and in our everyday lives, we are confronted with ideas, events, issues and so on, that are incongruent with our belief system. Initially we may reject the seemingly incongruent message. But over time, the sense which we failed to perceive initially, perhaps because of our use of denial, seeps through and we modify our ideas, beliefs and behaviour. The benefit, then, may occur at a much later time. The third important element in all of this, is that Mary may well have a belief that she has given help to John. This kind of belief may set up the possibility of of change in John, merely through the fact that Mary thought John worthy of 'faith'!

The fourth element in the statement - 'in $' - expresses the underlying values present in the helping situation. Both the helper and the client are carriers of culture, and the values inherent in their respective cultures. Not only that, but the very framework of 'helping' - eg. goals and processes - are themselves value-based and laden. Mary's refusal to help John rob a bank is an example of the possibility of the helper and the client having sets of values which may clash. The question is, can helping take place where helper and client values systems are in opposition? Helping is less likely to take place where underpinning value positions are inarticulated and/or ignored by both parties in the encounter.

There are other elements implicit in the statement 'Mary helps John' which have not been explored here. One example of this is the nature of the power relationship that exists between the parties, and the question of what it means to be a client or helper. The point of this analysis is to emphasise that inevitably the contact between helper and client is based on sets of assumptions, beliefs, and values, and that in our movement to self-conscious helping, these taken-for-granted 'rules' must be closely scrutinised. Failure to do so will tend to result in ineffective helping. The flow-diagram sets up in a systematic way, the stages in the process of helping, and an awareness of the overall, 'macro-picture' of helping can sharpen up the quality of our helping.

The movement to self-conscious helping can only be aided by having an understanding of what it means to be a client. In much of our research and teaching in counselling and helping, we have used mature students as clients. By and large, they report that their understanding of what it means to be a client has been heightened by the experience of being a client. Not only that, their counselling has, as a result, become that much more sensitive. Gilliland et al. (1984), believe that 'learning to be effective clients enhances our effectiveness as counsellors'. It is with this in mind that we now turn to the next chapter which focuses on what it means to be a client.

CHAPTER THREE

On Being a Client

3.1 Overview

What does it mean to be a client? This chapter will focus on the notion of clienthood, with the hope that due recognition by the helper of what it means to be a client will enable the helper to be more sensitive to, and caring about, the needs of the client. In discussing the nature of clienthood, we are inevitably sharpening the role of the helper.

Alan Keith-Lucas in discussing the 'art and science of helping', focuses on the nature of clienthood. He argues first of all, that all helping takes place in a relationship, and secondly, that people who come for help rarely really want to be helped.

To really ask for help makes demands on the client. It takes real courage to be a client - helpers must never become blase about working with clients; we should never take them for granted. An understanding of how a client becomes a client is important, and in the model proposed, it becomes obvious that once an individual embarks upon a career as a 'client', much of the ensuing movement into clienthood is outside the control of the individual. This may exacerbate existing feelings of powerlessness. An awareness of the career of 'client' also assists in our understanding of our role as helpers. This growing understanding of our role as helpers ought to aid our deepening recognition of what it means to be a client.

3.2 What it Takes to be a Client

What follows is an extract from a paper presented by Alan Keith-Lucas, and it directs our attention to the possibility that helping cannot take place outside a relationship, and that the reverse may also be true, that not all relationships are necessarily helpful. The other point of interest is his contention that people do not really want to be helped, but that in some way they really only want helpers to legitimate their own ideas, beliefs and actions. He also argues that 'real helping' is concerned with some kind of change. Change can be very threatening. The possibility of change may, however, be challenging, exciting and have a potential for personal growth.

For, despite the intuitive helping that some people seem to be able to do without, it seems, being taught, the vast majority of people go about helping most casually, confident somehow that if one only knows one's subject and gives the right kind of advice one has done all that one could, and that if the person we're helping doesn't take that advice, or do what we want him to, it is his plain and obvious fault. He's either stupid, or idle, or obstinate, or weak, and he ought to be punished for it - either by not getting any help, or by being starved, or shamed, or made to do what's right by some process or other - the law, or our inherent authority, or the pressure of public opinion, or argument, or having us take over his thinking for him, or a thousand different ways of putting pressure on him. Fortunately we have dispensed with the whip, at least for adults, the branding iron and the gallows as aids in the helping process, although all were used in the past. But one would have thought that our many failures should have shown us something else was wrong, that we had not somehow got hold of some basic principles, that there was more to it than that.

What then have we failed to see? I would like to start with two statements that may seem extremely simple but lie, I think, at the heart of the matter. The first is that all helping - all real helping, that is, the sort that really induces change - takes place in a relationship. And a relationship is a two-way thing. It matters as much what I put into it as what the other fellow does. What may go wrong with helping may be as much my fault as the helper, as it is may be on the part of the helped. The second is that people rarely really want to be helped.

This may sound like a strange statement, especially if one enlarges it, as I will, to include wanting to learn. It's true of course that many people profess an eager desire to learn. Others appear not only to ask for help but to demand it as if it were their right. But what these people profess to want, ask for, or even demand, is not real help or learning at all. It is help on their terms - help that will not force them to change in any way. It is in fact a way of warding off any real offer of help, a way of going through the motions, of pretending to oneself, of placating the gods, even, rather than really getting help.

Why might this be the case? Keith-Lucas suggests that perhaps we could understand this better if we realised what it really takes to ask for help. He believes it takes:

1. First of all the client has to recognise that there is something wrong, so wrong, that she cannot do anything about it by herself alone. For example, an alcoholic has first of all to acknowledge that he is an alcoholic, before he can be helped.

2. Secondly, the client has to have a willingness to confess this 'weakness' to another, to let him know what she really is. This is the process of self-disclosure, and it makes clients feel very vulnerable. It opens them up to ridicule, to censure, to judgement. A client has to feel safe in the relationship before she will be prepared to 'bare her soul' to this 'stranger'.

3. Whilst the baring of a soul to another is necessary, it is not really sufficient. Keith-Lucas considers that the client must then show a willingness to be advised. To allow this stranger to have some power over her life.

When we seek assistance, we place ourselves in the 'care' of others. One of the implications of being 'cared' for, is the abrogation of control to a lesser or greater degree. In our kind of society, there are those to whom, it is believed, it is legitimate and appropriate to give over control of the physical aspects of our functioning. So that if a person in 'authority' with all the trappings - white coat and stethoscope, for example - suggests something, we tend to go along with it. But our clients frequently find it difficult to accept counsel, particularly if it conflicts with currently held views. In the area of psychological and emotional functioning, it is harder to demonstrate expertness and there are fewer symbols of our 'authority'.

One of the problems for helpers, is to avoid the giving of advice. What needs to be done rather, in our opinion is to allow the client 'to advise herself'. This can be facilitated, for example, by the processes of clarification, confrontation, re-framing and getting the client to articulate possibilities (brain-storming is a good technique).

4. In addition to the three steps above, the client must finally consider a willingness to risk the unknown. To give up the present situation, however intolerable this may be, for some unknown that may look better

but may actually turn out worse requires real courage.

> Is it surprising, therefore, that people will do almost anything to prevent themselves from being helped? Is it surprising that many of them refuse to admit their real need, that they demand help from us on their own terms, that they find ways of neutralising our help? My students do it to me, and I expect your clients do it to you. One of the best ways, incidentally, of doing this is to agree with a great deal of literalness with what the helping person wants - to follow his advice blindly, and then be able to show him that what he advised did not work. Some of you, to be honest, will do this with what I have to say to you today and it will work to show me up. Another way is to go through all the motions yet somehow, somewhere, to miss the really important point, the thing that really matters - just as one of the best ways of not getting help from God is to go to church, to sing all the hymns, to be busy in 'church work' and never permit the essential message to get across. (Keith-Lucas, nd).

To a very great extent, it is risky to be a real client, because inherent in that role is the fact that the individual is in a process of change, and the helping we offer probably builds upon that process which, we believe, may have already started. The risk involved is not knowing what the end-product will be like. The risk centres upon the feelings of vulnerability within the client, and whether or not it is safe to trust the helper and, perhaps more importantly, the wondering by the client of whether or not they can trust themselves. Keith-Lucas also believes that clients are learners.

He fails to add that clients need also to be re-learners. Change implies the giving up of something old, and learning, doing, being something new. There is a sense in which the old has to be un-learned, and new ways re-learned. It is not surprising that clients (and all of us) tend to stick with what is known - the habitual, familiar ways of behaving. Giving up these old ways, are like giving up familiar friends, there are risks involved. That is why many clients, after trying like mad to change, frequently regress to older behaviours. Have you tried giving up smoking, or sticking to a diet? Some professional counsellor-trainers will not accept people into their counselling programmes unless they have or are willing to undertake some major change in their lives in line with the premise 'how can you expect clients to change, unless you have experienced change yourself!'

Clients also learn from us, and their learning is very rapid, particularly in picking up cues as to how to behave within the interview situation. Clients will learn from us what is appropriate to talk about, how to behave - whether for example to break down and cry in the interview, or to be serious, what attitudes and values to express, and so on. As workers we subtly indicate our beliefs, values and so on, and what is appropriate or not appropriate in interviews. Clients can also be forgiving, however, as the following extract indicates.

The following is a statement made by a client to a beginning counsellor, who was utilising a skills-training approach in a rather mechanistic fashion. Yet, the unspoken elements of caring and interest still came through.

> In most instances I knew you were going to say 'You feel such and such'. At first I was annoyed. I wanted much more than just feelings. I wanted you to tell me what to do, or yell at me, or tell me what I had done wasn't so bad. But you knew I didn't really need those things. After a while I started to appreciate the fact that you were really listening to me and caring for me. That made up for your limited responses. In later sessions, you did do other kinds of things, but it always was what occurred on a deeper basis which mattered. (Egan, 1976).

3.3 The Nature of Change

How do clients change? How do people change? Is change always perceptible, sudden and dramatic? Helpers need to have some understanding of the nature of change because the need for some kind of change is implicit in the client's coming for help. There are a number of ways in which change can be conceived. First of all, change can be conceived as arising from a struggle and a crisis within the client. Erikson (1963) considers that individuals pass through a number of crisis stages as they progress through the life-span. The successful resolution of the crisis at an earlier stage, sets the stage for successful resolution of stages at later points in the individual's life. If, however, a particular crisis is not well negotiated, there tends to be a carry-over into later stages, and there is inevitably a hampering of the resolution of later crises.

There are qualitative differences between the stages of many stage theorists so that change is manifested by a greater maturity in behaviour, differences in thinking, attitudes and so on. For example, the young person who has successfully negotiated Erikson's conflict of identity during adolescence, and who as a result has come to a tentative answer to the question 'Who Am I?' is in a favourable position to come to terms with the growth of 'intimacy', (the next stage) the sharing of self with others, without being threatened or fearing being swamped by the 'self' of the other. Note, that the identity resolution has to be tentative. This is not to say that there is a lack of confidence in who one is, but that there is a recognition of the possibility of growth and development, and change over the life-span. The identity crisis of adolescence does not disappear after adolescence, but returns in differing formats throughout the life-span. Who one is, for example, is heightened in true 'intimacy' with another, and thus, there is a further development of identity over the life-span.

Helpers need to be aware of changes that occur as a consequence of growing physical, emotional and intellectual maturity. A sound knowledge of human development is essential for all helpers, for any intervention by the helper may be impeded or facilitated by developmental change within the client. In addition, there are milestone events, or turning points which may have an impact on clients, and any intervention by helpers needs to take this possibility into account. For women, for example, childbirth may be such a significant event, as will the last child going to school. Many women choose to return to the careers or jobs that they held prior to having a family. Where the return occurs after a considerable time has elapsed, many women are dissatisfied with their positions, even though they are similar to those held previously. The big change is not so much in the job, but rather in the woman.

For men, critical points in their lives tend to revolve largely around career, though this might be changing. Many clients come to see us because of discontent or discomfort in their present lives. Sometimes, they find it extremely difficult to articulate this uneasiness, and it may be presented in interviews as 'whingeing', psychosomatically, or in some other form which bears little relationship to what is actually happening. If, as helpers you are aware of developmental changes that occur throughout the life-span, as well as those events which might be critical incidents or turning points, then your helping may be the more effective.

As helpers, we sometimes believe that clients can be changed in much the same way as Saul of Tarsus was changed on the road to Damascus. This is extremely unlikely. Tyler talks about minimum changes, which like the arc of a circle, increases as the angle remains the same, and the length of the radius increases. So much of the change that occurs as a result of helping, hopefully, has a wider and wider impact as time passes by. If the change is gradual, it may be difficult for the helper to be aware of it. For example, the man who needs to be assertive, but not aggressive may handle himself better at home or at work only once. The success of this may give him confidence to try it again. If success continues, the

35

frequency of his assertive behaviour may increase, and may have implications for all those with whom he has contact. Note, however, that because this kind of change affects others, the others may work to prevent your client from changing.

Watzlawick et al. (1974) considers that there are two major forms of change. One is 'first order' change, where change occurs in a system. Two examples might give the flavour of his ideas. Take, for example, a game of soccer (or any other game). The players may be moved around; there may be changes in the colour of the shirts and so on. Significant changes that occur in this context, have no effect on the nature of the game being played. The rules have not been changed. So that within the rules that have been established - the closed system - changes have occurred, but the game is the same. With our clients, they may make substantial and what apparently are significant changes in their behaviours and so on, but they may be playing the same kind of, for example, manipulative game in a different guise. The parameters of their activity have not really changed.

Second order change on the other hand, in essence, is concerned with changes to the rules, to use the analogies above. Change is exerted from outside the system. Watzlawick gives the example of a young couple who are doted on by parents to such an extent that the couple believe that they have no life of their own. This domination by parents extends to doing the shopping, and each week they insist on organising the shopping for the couple, and so on, with much protesting by the couple. Indeed the more the couple protested, the more the parents insisted on 'helping'. So Watzlawick then suggested the use of 'paradox' and that the couple should begin to insist on being helped by the parents. Thus changing quite dramatically the nature of the game. The couple were told by Watzlawick to be extravagant in their purchasing, and to fill the shopping trolley to the brim. The parents were aghast, and very quickly gave back to the couple their autonomy, particularly with regard to the shopping!

Helpers are in a unique position to be outside the 'game playing' by clients, and thus can suggest to clients possible solutions to intractable problems by the use of 'creative paradox'. One problem for helpers is that they frequently, because of a number of factors, become enmeshed in their clients' games, to the detriment of their practice and, of course, their clients.

Keith-Lucas suggested that many clients do not want to change, because among other things change requires courage and risk-taking. Many clients do want to change, but cannot appear to do so. The restraints on change appear to be greater than the encouragement required to facilitate change. Watzlawick's view is that this may be because of the nature of the crippling game that they are engaged in, and that rather than attempt to make first order change, what is really called for, is second order change. Helpers must be aware of the barriers to change, which may be within the client, but may well be within the system of relationships and ways of behaving that have emerged over time.

McCluskey (1970) is concerned with the capacity for change in that he envisages individuals having a 'margin of power over load'. That is, where individuals are confronted with change, it is important for helpers to ask questions about the capacity for change within the client. What are the resources available within the individual and his environment - psychological, emotional, physical, and so on - (power)? What kind of load is the client presently carrying? Is there any energy left for the client to make changes within her life? If there is not, then helpers do damage to clients by expecting and insisting that they change. It may be a more appropriate strategy on the part of the helper to insist on 'non-change'; upon consolidation, perhaps. Helpers need in this situation to offer support, such that clients can recoup their resources, so that in the future the client may be more enabled to make changes, if appropriate.

The notion of barriers to and facilitators of change emerges in a variety of formats. For example, Egan suggests that 'force-field analysis' (discussed later in the book) is a useful aid to decision making. Catastrophe Theory (Postle, 1980) highlights the suddenness and discontinuity of change. It is as though the individual has 'had enough', the final straw has broken the camel's back, and they are precipitated into change. There is continual tension between on the one hand, those aspects within the person and her environment which inhibit change, and on the other hand, those that are pushing towards a change. And seemingly, all of a sudden, something happens which confirms the need either for rapid change, or a continuation on the old course.

Much marital break-up takes this form. It is useful for the helper to look for the triggers which made the difference, and which prompted the change, even though change may have been under consideration for some time. Many clients become clients in this way. The courage or behaviour required to become a client somehow breaks through the inhibitory barriers - the threshold is broken and the client finds herself on your doorstep.

As helpers you must recognise and be aware of the ways in which clients become clients. The following section outlines a model, which is especially useful for understanding the client-making process.

3.4   How Does a Client Become a Client?

How does a client become a client or patient, and what happens to him in the process? The model which follows sets out the sequence of events from the behaviours or ideas which precipitate action, through the treatment phase, until discharge and return to the community. The model originally charted the process for a psychiatric patient, but the model has, in our opinion, wider applicability. It has been used to describe to teachers the punishment process within schools, and how, more often than not, a pupil who is punished for some allegedly heinous offence, is never really discharged or released from 'treatment' but is continually under surveillance, maybe even throughout the whole of his school career!

There are seven stages in this model of the 'unfolding career' of the client.

Stage 1   Primary Behaviour

The primary behaviour is that behaviour which draws attention to the individual. In the classroom situation it is difficult to decide whether the behaviour which the teacher 'acts upon' is in fact the first incident or the 'straw that breaks the camel's back'. Similarly, in the home situation, the final straw that precipitates action may be something rather insignificant, but frequently it is the culmination of a series of events which give it importance. Helpers have to be aware then, that the first incidents that their clients relate to them may in fact not be the real problems, but merely the events or incidents that led the client or his family to seek help. The 'presenting problem' may be a real problem, but not the most important one.

Stage 2   Reaction – Interpretation

Stage 2 occurs when the other person interprets this behaviour, having first noticed it. The other may decide to pass it by, to excuse or to rationalise its existence in some way or another. For example, in the classroom, primary behaviour may be excused if the teacher is aware, perhaps, that the pupil is suffering a grief reaction to a death in his immediate family. However, if the behaviour is perceived as a threat in some way to the teacher, or to some other individuals in the environment, then the teacher, or others observing the behaviour, may decide to 'do something about it'. (Note that the interpretation of the behaviour as threatening in some way is a function of the perceptions of the teacher or other observers, and does not necessarily reflect the intentions of the individual whose behaviour is in question).

Stage 3   Reaction – Decision

The decision to take some kind of action depends, then, on the behaviour being noticed and perceived in such a way that motivates the other to do something about it. The motivation to seek help may be because of threat to the other or perhaps a belief that harm may come to the individual. In other words, the seeking of help by the other for the individual may be because of felt needs within the other, or perceived needs of the individual by the concerned other.

Stage 4   Official Contact
Helpers must recognise that the decision by the other to hand the individual on to someone who can 'help', implicitly suggests that the other has some idea of what should happen to the individual. Teachers, for example, who hand on a pupil to the Deputy Principal rather than the counsellor within a school, are suggesting that the problem needs to be dealt with perhaps by punishment or other disciplinary action rather than by counselling. In other words, the decision to come to counselling help may be only one possibility in a range of possibilities, but one that is thought by the other, or by the client himself, to be appropriate, or safe!

It can happen that the wrong decision may be made - that is, the problem may not be amenable to counselling help of the kind offered by the helper's agency. The teacher who hands over the pupil to, say, the Deputy Principal, for punishment, may be hurt and very angry when the Deputy Principal just talks to the individual, and then sends him on his way. Many wives, for example, seek counselling help after being 'battered' by their husbands, failing to realise, perhaps, that the agency they should have gone to was the Police!

Stage 5   Treatment Decision
The decision to hand over to an official, means that the other has now to back out of the situation and leave the treatment decision to the official. Similarly, when the client of his own   volition comes to you as a helper, the suggestion is that the treatment decision lies in the hands of the helper. To a large extent this is true, but the model of helping presented as a flow-diagram in Chapter Two, points out that the treatment decision should, hopefully, be a joint decision of helper and client. In everyday helping situations, this has to be so because of the voluntary nature of the contact between client and helper.

In psychiatric institutions, prisons and schools, and other total institutions, however, the client is captive within a system, and the co-operation of the client in those situations may be neither necessary, nor sought by the officials. The duration, intensity, scheduling, and nature of the treatment tends to be in the hands of the official. Generally speaking, the treatment has the general concern to assist the individual in need - to modify his behaviour; to bring about a cure; to enable the individual to fulfil role-expectations; or whatever the goals are that the official prescribing the treatment has in mind. The assumptions here, of course, are that the official has expertise and knowledge, as well as the authority to prescribe the treatment. Helpers in voluntary agencies have the authority to prescribe treatment or offer assistance only to the extent that their clients allow this.

Stage 6   Release Decision

The decision to release from treatment is made by the official when he believes that the goals of the treatment have been reached. In schools, however, that release decision may not be given. The teacher may carry on his 'vendetta', even after the pupil has been the subject of disciplinary action. In helping situations, care has to be taken to release the client from treatment. Some helpers may in fact perpetuate relationships with clients because of their own unresolved needs. However, the model of the helping process, presented earlier, should alert helpers to this possibility and to the need to carefully evaluate the clients and their own behaviour.

Stage 7   Community Adaptation

The last stage in the model points up the need for the helper to be aware that the client lives in a community -   that the client is part of a family, classroom, town, city, and so on. Research evidence consistently points to the fact that where families are 'prepared' for the return home of family members from psychiatric institutions the success rate is higher than when no preparatory work has been conducted. Helpers must never forget that their clients live within a complex nexus of relationships outside of the counselling or helping relationship, and that these relationships are likely to be powerful forces within the client's life.

The loss of control that many patients feel in the hospital, or in other settings, is amply demonstrated in this model. For it is the reactions of others that play a crucial role in the unfolding career of a client in all stages, except perhaps the first!

The model sets out the likely steps in the careers of a client or patient. Helpers must be aware of the events or incidents that precipitated the client's seeking help. And, as has previously been mentioned, helpers must be aware that, possibly, the initial problems outlined by the client may not in fact be the most important, but may mask the important issues that are concerning the client. Furthermore, helpers must be aware not only of the ambivalence of clients but that clients often feel powerless once enmeshed in the process of becoming and being a client. Keith-Lucas describes what it means to be a client, and an understanding of clienthood should make the helper more aware and sensitive to the fears, anger, and sorrow exhibited by many clients.

Have you ever been a patient in a hospital? Think of the ways in which the institution robs the individual of his individuality! Recently my brother-in- law had to go into hospital for observation. He was told that he had no need to go to bed; that is, he could stay up and walk around. It was a fine warm day, but 'would he mind wearing pyjamas', because then he could be identified as a patient!

Cumming and Cumming (1962), in their research studies into psychiatric hospitals in the United States, showed how the very processes of receiving in-patients into the hospital studied, increased the disorientation of many patients. The processes in fact set up a self-fulfilling prophecy - 'they are in hospital because they are mad'. Thereafter, the prophetic statement could be justified by reference to the confused behaviour of the patient at the time of entry into the psychiatric hospital!

What happens, then, is that the individual is cast into a role - that of 'patient'- which has built into it a series of expectations of how patients or clients ought to behave. When, at times, patients or clients do not fit in with these expectations, this may cause difficulties for helpers and clients alike. Sometimes, the client's attempts to be a client may be rejected. In one study, patients in a psychiatric institution had symptoms which did not fit in with the expectations of nurses. The nurses had been led to expect symptoms A, B, and C from patients diagnosed as ...'X'. When, however, patients exhibited symptoms other than A, B, or C, they were either discharged as 'cured', or placed in the back-wards of the institution. Similar difficulties have been experienced by those caring for dying patients, (Mauksch, 1975).

The role of client involves a complex set of behaviours which generally includes having to be dependent, being subservient and is usually associated with a significant loss in power, status and perceived competence. The following comments from a client highlight the some of the feelings associated with clienthood.

> ...when given a public charity, you somehow become the lowest form of life in everyone's eyes, even the rest of the poor. It is there in (their) attitudes, and it is not imagined. (Colin, 1974: 40)

> ...I did feel I was losing my self-respect, and none of the Board's officers at any time said or did anything that might make me change that view. (Colin, 1974: 49)

> Guilt poured over me. But what had I done? Did I have to be

punished forever for being poor? Even criminals don't have life sentences now... (Colin, 1974: 158)

Helpers have to be careful that their very training does not incapacitate them in their work with clients. Trained incapacity refers to the fact that whilst training may provide the helper with a set of blinkers or lenses through which to view the world, they may blind the helper from seeing the client as he really is. Helpers need to realise that clients have 'histories' and that these include developed ways of coping with the world that may or may not be susceptible to change. The longer an habitual way of behaving has been in use, the longer might be the required time to effect some kind of change.

Client are the 'consumers' of the help we offer. They will tend to structure their behaviour in order to ensure that their needs are met. This may result in bizzare behaviour; behaviour that shocks, or in over-compliance with worker demands. If their needs are not met, then it is highly likely that the client will go elsewhere. This may be threatening to helpers in agencies whose funding is derived from the number of clients 'on the books'. So whilst it is important to recognise that clients suffer a diminution in power, this does not necessarily mean that they are powerless! Nor is it totally true, as suggested by the model of the 'unfolding career' of the client, that clients cannot control the character of the decisions being made about them.

One of our clients was in serious difficulties with the police for using explosives on a brewery! He had been told by his mates that, if he ever got into serious trouble, he ought to 'plead insanity' because life in a psychiatric institution was much more pleasant than being in prison!

The analysis of clienthood offered in this chapter should not deter the helper from asking questions about the identity of the 'real' client. Families and others may push forward clients as symptoms of wider pathology in the family, institution, or society. Many of our clients are victims; many play the 'victim' role very well. As helpers, we need to be aware of the stigma of being a client, and to recognise that as a consumer of our helping, clients have a role in 'quality control'; their perceptions of what is happening to them, inside them, may be the best indicators of the effectiveness of our helping.

It is important to realise, too, that as helpers we are dealing with people who, more often than not, perceive themselves as failures. Our recognition of this perception, together with the acceptance of the ambivalence and anxiety that are inevitably present within the client may make us more tolerant of the anger and hostility which may be poured in our direction. The resolution of ambivalence, and the need to dissipate the anxiety, are strong motivators for change, and helpers ought to be able to capitalise on this in the helping process. Maybe, if we take seriously Sir James M. Barrie's statement, we may be sensitive enough to help our clients:

We are all of us failures - at least the best of us are.

CHAPTER FOUR

The Person of the Helper

4.1 Overview

In this chapter, the focus is upon you, the helper - one of the basic ingredients of the helping process. To a very large extent, the quality of the helping depends upon the person offering the help. We have noted earlier that helping can be for 'better or worse' and our concern is that people who are offering themselves as helpers ought to be the best available. We certainly would not want incompetent, inadequate people puddling around in our affairs, with gumboots on! We have indicated that for us, helper self-awareness is extremely important, and is a part of the helper's armamentarium. It seems to make sense to suggest that if you are not aware of or sensitive to yourself as a person, or how you function and affect other people, it is unlikely that you will be sensitive to the needs and feelings of others!

4.2 Self-Awareness and Mental Health

The following extract from Don Hamachek's (1978) 'Encounters with the Self' sets out some of our beliefs about the relationship between self-awareness and mental health. He argues that our feelings about ourselves are learned responses. In the last chapter, it was pointed out that our clients are learners, and that not only may they have to un-learn behaviours, beliefs, attitudes and so on, but they may also have to re-learn in order to make the kinds of changes that they want. This is a challenge, for them and for us. An additional point is that our clients learn from us, and if, by our attitudes, behaviours and so on towards them, we can enable them to regard themselves as healthy in Hamachek's terms, then perhaps the need for our services will dissipate.

> Healthy people see themselves as liked, wanted, acceptable, able and worthy. Not only do they feel that they are people of dignity and worth, but they behave as though they were. Indeed, it is in this factor of how people see themselves that we are likely to find the most outstanding differences

between high and low self-image people. It is not the people who feel that they are liked and wanted and acceptable and able who fill our prisons and mental hospitals. Rather, it is those who feel deeply inadequate, unliked, unwanted, unacceptable, and unable. Research is showing that self-acceptance and personal happiness has a lot to do with accepting others and enjoying what one is and what one has, maintaining a balance between expectations and achievements.

Self and self-other understanding are not mystical ideals standing someplace 'out there' as unreachable goals. Social feeling, empathic listening, honesty, and an understanding of how we use our defense mechanisms are all ways to assist in the development of greater self-awareness and self-understanding. Our feelings about ourselves are learned responses. Sometimes bad feelings have to be unlearned and new feelings acquired. This is not always easy, but it is possible. Sometimes this means 'taking stock' of oneself - a kind of personal inventory. Or it may mean baring one's self to another person - a friend or therapist - so that the possibility for honest evaluation and feedback is more probable. And for certain, it means changing those things which one can and accepting those which one cannot.

For most persons, a positive, healthy self-image is quite within reach if they are willing to accept the risks and responsibilities for mature living and if they know how to go about it.

If, as parents or as professional persons, we have a basic understanding of how a healthy self is developed and the conditions and interpersonal relations which nurture it, then we are in a position to move actively in the direction of creating those conditions and interpersonal relationships most conducive to positive mental health.

Perhaps the best place to begin is with ourselves. (Hamachek, 1978).

A great deal has been written about the self; the development and maintenance of self-esteem and the building of an identity within which we are confident and secure. George Herbert Mead, one of the great social philosophers of this century, described a concept of the self which we believe has some implications for helpers. The self, according to Mead

45

has two aspects - the 'I' and the 'me'. The self, then, can be both 'subject' and 'object'. The 'I' is that part of the self which is active in doing, being, and feeling, for example, in the here-and-now; in the existential present. It is that part of the self that becomes engaged with the world. The 'me' on the other hand looks at the self as object and asks questions about the happenings in the moment-by-moment living. 'How did I do?'; 'What else could I have done?'; 'I wonder why I felt this way when...?'. So for Mead, the 'me' is the reflective, introspective part of the self, which asks questions of the 'I'.

In reality of course, the picture is more complicated than that, because in the moment-to-moment reflecting about the 'I', the 'me' in fact becomes the 'I' and is itself capable of being reflected upon. There are many expressions of this kind of idea, and in the writings of R.D. Laing there are some especially intriguing examples as the following extract shows:

> There must be something the matter with him
> because he would not be acting
> as he does unless there was
> therefore he is acting as he is
> because there is something the matter with him
>
> He does not think there is anything the matter with him
> one of the things that is
> the matter with him
> is that he does not think there is anything
> the matter with him
> therefore
> we have to help him realise that,
> the fact that he does not think there is anything
> the matter with him
> is one of the things that is
> the matter with him   (Laing, 1970)

As an object of awareness, the self inevitably incorporates the responses of others to the 'I'. The self according to Mead is socially formed, and can only arise in social settings where there is some kind of interaction. 'He becomes a self in so far as he can take the attitude of another and act toward himself as others act.' (Mead, 1934). The rules by which we respond characteristically to the reactions of others to the 'I' become, over time the roles we play. Roles are really governed by sets of rules that guide behaviour within certain contexts or settings. Thus, the actor within a role, the 'I' has the freedom to take initiative, to be free. The quality of the performance within the role can only take place upon completion of the performance.

In helping, the 'I' is active in the interview in encountering the client. The 'me' is able to reflect on how well the 'I' did, in the heat of the exchange with the client. Good counsellors do not wait until the completion of the interview for the 'me' to be reflective on the process. It becomes part and parcel of 'the role' where the helper is continually asking questions of his performance in relation to what is happening to the client. The process of helping should have this kind of 'self-reflective' activity built-in as a conscious and purposeful component. For helpers, this kind of self-awareness, and the introspection required to go on examining and monitoring their own feelings, responses, attitudes and behaviours is as much a part of the helping process as is the interaction with the client.

We need to be self-aware, and frequently it helps to give ourselves guidelines for the asking of those reflective type questions. To this end we have included some ideas from Simpson (1976), who raised a number of questions which, he believed, even experienced counsellors ask themselves, provided they have not become rigid in their thinking.

4.3   Some Questions for People Interested in Counselling Others
It is important for helpers to continually ask themselves questions about the 'what', 'how' and 'why' of their involvement in helping. Whilst there is some overlap, the questions have been grouped under four broad headings. You may be able to think of other questions that helpers should ask of themselves!

(a)   "Why are you here" Questions:
What are your motives for wanting to help others? Should you be considering counselling? Are you physically fit enough and emotionally stable enough to help anyone? Are you hoping that counsellor training will solve your own personal problems? Do you need counselling yourself? What do you expect to learn from a course or study in counselling? Whatever are you going to try to do to and for people with what you learn?

(b)   Conceptual Questions:
Do you think of helping as enabling others to 'adjust' to life? Do you think of helping people to 'gain independence'? (Each such approach suggests its own conceptual assumptions about the world, about human nature, and counselling method.) Do you talk of 'solving problems', or of 'giving advice', or of 'treating' people? Or, in the age of Skinner, of 'modifying or changing behaviour'? Or are you more psychoanalytically oriented? Do you talk of helping people to 'understand'? Have you been

in some (fashionable) sensitivity or encounter groups, and think of 'being real' or helping people to 'grow' or to 'self-actualise'? These terms stand for concepts that imply very different ways of working with people.

(c) Personal Quality Questions:

What are the qualities which you believe might enable you to help others? Do you have any such qualities? Are they the same qualities that make for a good wife and mother, or husband and father? Or do you need a degree in psychology? Or medicine? Or theology? Do you need to have certain personal values? Or have a certain kind of personality? Or do you need to hold certain attitudes toward people? Or to have had certain experiences? How important is experience? (Some of our most muddled clients have raised the largest families!) Is 'plain practical commonsense' as invaluable as many people believe? Finally, how important are frankness, honesty, respect for people, awareness of self and others, or empathy?

(d) Theory or Strategy Questions:

What is your theory of helping others? What is your view of a healthy effective person? Can you distinguish normal from abnormal people? How do you view your responsibility toward those you seek to help? Do you help some and not others? What about the prostitute who seeks an abortion? Or the homosexual with orgasm problems? Would you want to help them? Who will you want to refuse, refer on, or help? More fundamentally perhaps, have you a theory of learning? How do you think people learn? Or relearn? How can you help them to change?

4.4 Some Criteria for the Selection of Helpers

Simpson (1976) has also outlined some criteria for counsellor selection. You might like to consider, adopt or adapt some of these for the selection of helpers in your agency. You may also consider whether or not you 'fit the bill'!

1. Are you acceptable to people on personal grounds, such as honesty, considerateness, tact, informality?

2. Are you sensitive to or aware of various human problems, and willing to discuss them, rather than preach about them?

3. Are you open-minded about people dissimilar to yourself, tolerant of their behaviour and values, and of their attempts, even if awkward, to cope with life?

4. Are you willing to become involved in the problems of people, to listen and help?

5.   Are you willing to share your own experiences? Clients, especially adolescents, value people who say what they believe, rather than sit on the fence. Moral neutrality is, especially for the adolescent, a pose.

6.   Are you competent and comfortable in your own occupation and life?

7.   Are you 'human'? Can you show human feelings? To many people, emotion is the enemy of reason, and is something to be repressed.

8.   Do you have a sense of proportion in your own morality? Does strange dress, long hair, or minor delinquency, anger or upset you greatly?

9.   Do you believe in people? In the inherent worth of every individual, and in the potential each individual has to improve his situation if helped?

10. Are you curious about the world, social change, and people? Do you seek, by introspection, or reading, or other experiences to increasingly understand the complex world you live in?

11. Can you be responsible? Or might you seduce a client and tell yourself it was a 'growth experience' for both of you? Do you have the personal integrity to withstand the subtle human pressures of counselling?

12. How will you respond to those from different ethnic and minority groups? What is your reaction to Aboriginality; to Asians; to those from the Pacific Islands; to members of the opposite sex?

Embedded within some of these questions are some cues as to the kinds of values and attitudes which, we believe, are appropriate and are pre-requisites for helpers. Values such as respect for the dignity and worth of others, belief in the capacity of individuals to change and to enhance their lives, acceptance and respect for ethnic and cultural differences amongst people. These are values issues for us, and we are continually testing out our beliefs and values against the realities that confront us in our work, and our personal lives.

4.5   Self-Description and Self-Disclosure

Self-awareness has been described as a crucial ingredient in helping. It is suggested, among other things, that 'good mental health' is a function of an individual's self-awareness. Certainly, it is to be hoped that you as helpers, in general, tend to be healthier than your clients, or you may find your client counselling you! There are a number of ways in which we

49

can heighten our self-awareness. Firstly, helpers can be asked to describe themselves, and then to have their perceptions of themselves checked out by others. This can be achieved for example, by the use of lists of traits or characteristics which can be checked or by the use of responses to questions such as 'Who Am I? What Am I in relation to my family, my community, my country and so on?'

Secondly, we can ask helpers to self-disclose something that they have not revealed before, and to reflect upon what happened when that occurred! Thirdly, our self-awareness can be increased by the use of constructive, accurate feedback about our performance, our behaviour, our attitudes. This may be risky, in that the feedback we receive, may be not what we want or appreciate.

The fourth way in which we can learn something about ourselves is to be self-conscious about risk-taking, trying out new behaviours and roles, just to discover how we react in these novel situations.

Self-description
In a very real way, the Who or What Am I? exercise is an attempt at self-description. The answers we give to the question generally reflect some of the feelings and ideas we have about our physical characteristics, the roles we play, our effectiveness as a person, and so on. The difficulty with self-description is that it may not be a true or accurate description. Obviously, with our physical features - height, weight, colour of hair and eyes, etc, we can be assured that our description is fairly accurate; similarly, with our qualifications, and the jobs and roles we play. But when we start to ask questions about how effective we are in the roles that we perform, or how we physically affect other people, the descriptions we give of ourselves in these areas are more ambiguous, and more open to self-deception. Some people seem to find the need to paint good pictures of themselves, others self-deprecate themselves; some are like Uriah Heep, ostensibly 'ever so humble'.

These masks we take on are, in a very real sense, the descriptions we want others to have of us. To this extent, we are a little Machiavellian, frequently engaged in 'impression management', for the purpose of, among other things, self-protection.

Further, and unfortunately again, the impression of ourselves which we think we are giving to other people, may be misunderstood by them. A person who believes he is being modest may be seen by others as 'crawling to the boss'. Or a person who believes he is giving a confident and accurate account of his qualifications and experience may be seen by others as being arrogant. There are then, hazards in self-descriptions, because they are always open to interpretation and mis-interpretation by others. Self-descriptions are in a very real sense public knowledge. Self-disclosure, on the other hand, implies the giving of information to others which normally they do not have.

Self-disclosure

Self-disclosure is seen by Jourard (1971) as the ability of the individual to make himself known to at least one other significant being.

> When I say that self-disclosure is a means by which one achieves personality health, I mean that it is not until I am my real self that my real self is in a position to grow. . . People's selves stop growing when they repress them. . . Alienation from one's real self not only arrests personality growth; it tends to make a farce of one's relationships with people. (Jourard, 1971)

Self-disclosure is a risk, an act of faith, that whatever you disclose will be treated with respect and dignity by other people; that people will not mock you. Self-disclosure, however, goes somewhat further than this, in that it allows the articulation of those things which are feared. It brings out those hidden elements for self and public scrutiny. The woman, who for example, has a secret fear that the lump in her breast may be cancer, may go to extraordinary lengths not to reveal it to loved ones, or even to her physician. She may deny its existence, or rationalise its evidence in a variety of ways, yet at the same time fearing that if it were admitted, allowed to exist, almost, then she may have to tackle the larger problem of cancer.

Such people if allowed to self-disclose gain enormous relief. Frequently, the fears when confronted tend to disappear and we are left wondering why we did not self-disclose earlier. The very positive gains obtained from self-disclosure are a very real danger for the helper in his efforts to help the client for, as Egan (1976) points out, in the helping process self-disclosure is not an end in itself. That is, it has purpose, and that purpose is to aid the client. Inappropriate self-disclosure by the helper may change the nature of the helping relationship and damage the client.

Self-disclosure can be viewed along a number of useful dimensions, and the appropriateness of any self-disclosure can be ascertained by examining it in relation to these dimensions suggested by Egan (1976).

The dimensions of self-disclosure are:

1. breadth: the amount of information disclosed;

2. depth: the intimacy of information disclosed;
3. duration: the amount of time spent in disclosing oneself;
4. target person: the person or persons to whom information is disclosed;
5. the nature of the relationship: intimate friends, close friends, acquaintances, work associates, and so forth; and
6. situation: the conditions under which the disclosure is made.

Obviously, various combinations of the dimensions listed above are possible. For instance, a person who is constantly talking about himself (duration) and who reveals a great deal (breadth) of superficial information (depth) to almost anyone (random target person) on almost any occasion (situation) is usually called a 'bore', and shunned.

Cozby (1973) approaches the question of appropriateness in self-disclosure by hypothesising the differences between the self-disclosure of well-adjusted people and that of poorly adjusted people. The well-adjusted person, he suggests, engages in relatively high-level or significant self-disclosure, in terms of breadth (amount) and intimacy (depth), to a few significant others (spouse, very close friends), while being moderately self-disclosing to others in his immediate social environment (friends with whom he is less close, social acquaintances). 'Moderate' self-disclosure means that the well-adjusted person will disclose enough to establish meaningful social bonds but not enough to be threatening or offensive.

On the other hand, the poorly adjusted person either 'overdiscloses' or 'underdiscloses' (in terms of both breadth and depth) to virtually everyone in the environment. Poorly adjusted people have difficulty adapting self-disclosure to different kinds of target persons and different situations. The husband who says little about himself or what he does (breadth) to his wife (target person), finds intimate disclosure (depth) to almost anyone impossible. And, if he cannot share himself even moderately when his wife shares herself deeply with him (situation), he would fall into the 'poor adjustment' category.

Feedback
Feedback, if accurate and constructive can be a very powerful way of further understanding the way we relate to the world. For feedback to be useful there must be a receptivity within us that allows us, without undue defensiveness to listen carefully to other people and to consider in a very careful way the feedback offered.

It constantly amazes us that it is easy for us to receive feedback from the environment, where the environment is neutral, and as a result modify our behaviour accordingly. When we drive a car, for example, we are constantly receiving feedback about how well we are doing, and the more skilled we are, the more carefully are we in touch with our performance behind the wheel of our car. We can for instance, keep a constant speed if required; accelerate out of trouble, and corner and brake under the appropriate conditions. Yet, in many situations, we find it difficult to accept feedback on our performance as human beings. We love the feedback from our children, perhaps, because of their spontaneity, but tend to be extremely cautious of feedback from peers, maybe our partner, and others in the human environment. How many times, for example, do you deprecate a compliment that you have received? Or does it, like self-disclosure, depend on the nature of the circumstances, who the giver was, the situation, its depth and so forth?

It is extremely important for the client to receive accurate, caring constructive feedback from helpers. Recognise though, that the client, like us, may tend to disregard it, or handle the feedback inappropriately in some way or other. Remember also, that the feedback you give as helpers, may be the first accurate constructive feedback that the client has received for a very long time. In a very real sense, clients are clients because of the inappropriateness of the feedback received in the past, or the inappropriate interpretations given by clients to the feedback received.

Risk-taking
Keith-Lucas argued that clients need courage to be clients, because part of being a real client involves envisaging the possibility of change and being prepared to take the risks involved. As helpers, we have to be risk-takers, not in the sense of gambling, or being reckless, but more in the sense of being open to the possibility of being flexible enough to try out new experiences for their intrinsic worth. Many men, for example going through the mid-life transition, try themselves out on a completely new range of activities, from the first parachute jump, to learning something new, making new contacts, developing new hobbies and so on. Risk-taking involves a deep-seated curiosity about the world and our role in it, trying it out for size and then reflecting upon the experiences, in the Meadian sense!

The four ingredients that contribute to enhanced self-awareness: self-description; self-disclosure; feedback; and risk-taking, are encapsulated within a model which has been called the Johari Window. The model indicates what might be meant by being healthy, and what it is that we expect of our clients. We expect them to self-disclose; we expect them to receive feedback and use it well (especially if given by us!); to take risks and to widen their own knowledge of themselves through self-description.

We have no right, we believe, to demand of our clients that which we are not prepared to demand of ourselves. We have no right to demand growth and change from our clients when we have atrophied in our relationships to self and to others!

4.6 The Johari Window

The Johari Window summarises all the information that is available to be known about a person (Luft, 1969). Knowledge or information which is known about an individual can be broken into two areas - that knowledge which is known to the individual self, and that knowledge which is not.

Known to Self	Unknown to Self

Similarly, revelation can be divided into two areas, that which is known to others - ie. that which we have revealed to another, and that information we have not revealed.

Known to Others
Not Known to Others

When the two diagrams are merged we obtain a total picture of our 'knowledge' relationship to others in four Cells, thus:

The Johari Window

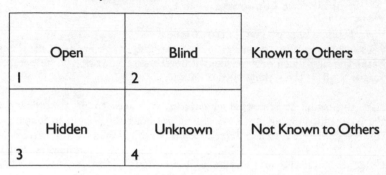

The size of any one of the Cells is dependent upon the size of the other Cells. The more we can acknowledge and reveal of ourselves, the larger will be Cell 1. One way of viewing the helping process is to argue that Cell 1 ought to be as large as possible, for this is the Cell which indicates the degree of knowledge about the self, which is open to the self and to others. Knowledge in this Cell is within the control of the individual, giving them power over their lives. It becomes important, throughout the helping process to enable the client to move material from Cells 2, 3 and 4 into Cell 1 – the Cell in which they have the power and the control.

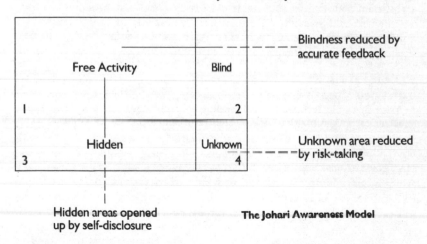

The Johari Awareness Model

55

Self-knowledge increases as we move material from Cell 3 to Cell 1. Similarly, if we receive accurate feedback from other people, this will also have the effect of increasing the area of Cell 1. The knowledge that the client is enabled to obtain by feeling 'safe' enough to take risks, moves material from Cell 4 into Cell 1.

4.7   Implications of the Johari Window

The assumption within the model is that the larger the area of Cell 1, the greater the likelihood of good mental health. Presumably, the helper has a larger Cell 1 than that of the client.

Whilst the model is somewhat simplistic, it seems to us to present a picture of what helping is about. It is about enabling people to take more effective control over their lives. This is accomplished by the moving of material from Cells 2, 3, and 4 into Cell 1. The assumption here is that if individuals have the information and knowledge, the facts (including ideas about the rules which control behaviour), then they are more likely to be in control of their lives. The model assumes that the lines which divide the Cells are straight lines, but this need not be the case. For example, one piece of self-disclosure may have a quite disproportionate impact upon the area of 'free activity', and this may have a cumulative effect over time.

The Johari Window presents a process model, but does not have a time dimension, which is a pity. Perhaps the model should be drawn in three dimensions! Another criticism of the model relates to the notion of the 'others'. The apparent assumption is that it does not matter who the others are! This is patently untrue, since the self-disclosure of significant material to non-significant others may not produce the kind of changes which might be expected. Similarly, the way in which we handle feedback depends to a very large extent on who is giving the feedback. The model ignores this aspect.

While the Johari Window has some utility, it also has, like all models, its deficiencies and limitations. Nonetheless, we believe that beginning helpers can gain from an understanding of the model. It is apparent, for example, that the quality of the communication between helper and client is crucial in enabling the movement of material into Cell 1, and this will be explored further in the next chapter. In fact, it could be even argued that good mental health results from receiving good accurate feedback from other people. If our perceptions of ourselves fit in with the perceptions of other people; if there is congruence between what we believe about ourselves and what other people believe about us, then, perhaps, we are in a position to enjoy good mental health. The fact is, unfortunately, that a great many people are impoverished by a lack of honest feedback about themselves; their personality and their behaviour. This impoverishment distorts contact between people, creating further vulnerability, mistrust, and a continuing lack of openness to experiencing life, in an ever downward spiral. You may care to read the poem - **(4.10) Who is the You Nobody Knows,** which continues to have an impact on us!

Helping through counselling should provide a new kind of relationship, characterised by caring, honest feedback, which would enable clients to allow the movement of material from Cell 2 to Cell 1 in the Johari Window. The trust and respect engendered in the helping relationship should, in time, enable those things which have been hidden to be exposed, by movement of material from Cell 3 to Cell 1, and allow the client to begin to take the risks so necessary for satisfying living.

This discussion of the nature of self-awareness, and the considerable extent to which it is demanded of helpers, would seem, perhaps, to confront helpers (and would-be helpers) with a pretty tall order. The requirement to be well-adjusted, self-aware, sensitive to the needs and requirements of self and others, and to be functioning in daily life at a healthier, more stable and enriched level than that of clients, would seem too much to expect. The extent of personal and professional commitment required is correspondingly substantial. So, you may well ask,'why should I get involved in this? Why should I place myself in a situation - a profession - where such effort and commitment is seemingly a prerequisite, and may be beyond me?' Why indeed!

There may be some answers for you in your own responses to the 'why am I here?' questions set out earlier in this chapter. Or, in your completing a Johari Window, in which you indicate areas in which you would like some feedback, and some of those things which you are now prepared to disclose, which previously you were unable to. There may also be some answers for you reflected in the views of others, especially in relation to the commitment of helpers to their profession.

The reasons for the continued influx of people into the helping professions, and their ability to continue to function, have been of interest to many writers. Why and how do people in the helping professions continue to function in working environments which offer, characteristically:

1. little concrete verifiable evidence of 'success';
2. a minimum of feedback;
3. notoriously poor salary and conditions, (including long hours, and an expectation of dedication well beyond the 'call of duty');
4. significant doses of frustration, especially in relation to any one

worker's potential to make any real impact upon the welfare of individuals and society?

Considering that helpers are required to engage in the development and maintenance of self-awareness at a very demanding level, which in terms of the Johari Window, suggests continuous movement of material into Cell 1, it is worth looking at some of the ideas which have been put forward to account for the almost bizarre persistence of these professional helpers in such situations. Part of this obviously is a function of the needs of the helper, as exemplified in the earlier 'Mary helps John' discussion.

4.8   Halmos, Biestek, and the Mystery of the Surviving Helpers

In his 1957 work, 'The Casework Relationship', Felix Biestek conceives an inspired and dedicated individual, attracted to 'welfare' work by the highly idealistic value base of the helping professions. This individual, however, is beset by conflicts inherent in the helping enterprise, and has to juggle many a paradox in order to survive. For example, Biestek characterises the worker as both a 'firm-footed realist' and a 'clear-eyed idealist' (1957):

> As a realist, the caseworker is expected to see, understand, and help with the hard, sometimes ugly and repulsive realities in the lives of his clients. As an idealist, the caseworker is expected to recognise in a practical way the dignity and nobility of people who, in some instances, may have lost respect for themselves.

> As an idealist, the caseworker is the champion of the rights of individuals. As a realist, he is aware that individual rights are limited by the rights of   other individuals and by the common good of society.

> As an idealist he understands the importance of the emotional component in the lives of people who are in trouble; as a realist, he knows that emotional needs and problems, important as they may be, are not the most important considerations in human living. Without imposing his own standards and values upon clients, he tries to help them remain within objective social, legal, and moral boundaries.
> (Biestek, 1957)

These statements are an expression of the conflicting and dualistic modes of thinking required in helping. They are compatible with a great many similar observations throughout philosophy and psychology, as well as in religious teachings. Paul Halmos (1965) has reviewed the paradoxes inherent in helping, and believes that the dissonance of ideas is a state of mind that could be conducive to creative thinking and faithful dedication to the task. Biestek's statements, above, present to us both conflicting and competing value positions: that is, indeed, dissonance. So, how does the juggler juggle? Well, for Biestek's worker, there is a consolation for the burdensome juggling act. It lies in the divine inspiration accompanying and underlying the worker's practice:

> As an idealist, he sees each client as a precious child of the heavenly father. As a realist, he sees the client as he really is, with attitudes and behaviour which perhaps are quite unlike to God's. With the motive of love, he strives for skill in the use of the wisdom of sciences to help his brother in need. The caseworker hopes that he is, in some small way, an instrument of Divine Providence. (Biestek, 1957)

This emphasis upon the inspiration of Christianity in welfare work is not unique to Biestek. It is, to some degree, consistent with what Halmos calls the 'faith' of the helping professionals. Halmos believes that the

> . . . refrainlike acceptance of contradictory propositions, and incompatible canons of technique is a characteristic of counselling ideology which hallmarks the counsellor's faith. . . (Halmos, 1965).

It bears closer examination.

Faith in the Face of Paradox

The attribution of 'faith' constitutes Halmos' answer, in part, to the question 'How is the helper's role possible?'. This implies, amongst other things, that the helping role is not possible without some almost other-worldly rationale or motivating force. Halmos regards 'the counsellors' (including psychiatrists, lay and medical psychotherapists, clinical psychologists, social workers and welfare workers), as a new 'social factor' in our society. He believes that the emergence of the professions of secular counselling in the twentieth century is related to the decline of the social significance of the Christian interpretation of social and individual welfare, which has accompanied the age of modern science. He views secular personal services as essentially acting in lieu of the spiritual consultants of former times. Hence, the notion of 'faith' derives from those times, and has been retained as a necessary component in the effective practice of personal service.

Faith does not come under the rubric of skills which can be learnt, any more than does empathy, although skill in its transmission to a client can be enhanced with training. Halmos' strongest argument for the presence of faith in the counsellor is in his discussion of the paradoxes inherent in the helping task. They are summarised here:

> 1. The paradox of spontaneity combined with strategy - the irony of prescribing spontaneity needs no comment. In spite of that irony, according to Halmos, helpers recognise that their helping is more effective when it is carried out with spontaneous warmth and caring in association with a well planned strategy.

> 2. The paradoxical belief in the ultimate rationality and the pervasive irrationality of human nature. Halmos has observed that. . . 'the counsellor believes in the all pervasiveness of the impulsive, the emotional, and of the so-called Id forces of life, yet he is a firm believer, too, in the supreme rationality and intelligence of life'.
> (1965: 158)

One intriguing aspect of this paradox is the question of applying rationally-conceived strategies to the emotional irrationality of client problems. A besieged helper may indeed build up a psychological storehouse of skills, techniques, strategies, and methods, in order to ward off the infectious panic of anxious clients. . . great caseloads of them. The extent to which this storehouse also numbs the worker to the capacity to be spontaneously responsive to the distressed client is the area of interface between rational and irrational modes of operating.

> 3. The paradox of modelling non-directive morality - There is an essential irony in the counsellor being in control of the helping process, while at the same time aiming to show the client that the client is 'in charge' of both the purposes of the process and indeed, hopefully, his own life.

> 4. The paradox of scientific honesty - taking on the profession of helping implies that the helper is in some respects different (better?) to natural helpers in the community. The difference must be seen to lie in the acquisition of skills, knowledge and techniques through publicly recognised formal training programmes. But since it is part of that training to acknowledge the significance of intuition and personally held beliefs, values and attitudes, the helper must accommodate this part of herself with the 'applier of science' image created by a wealth of training.

5. The paradox of treatment without end. The historical tendency to emulate the medical model of treatment is foiled by the fact that the 'treatment' offered by counsellors has no finite end point, as in curing a disease. One never really knows whether the 'treatment' is finished or successful, or even at times, appropriate or relevant.

4.9 The Creative Paradox

Halmos' suggestion that the paradox-engendered state of mind tends to be most creative has already been mentioned. That is, cognitive dissonance can be a creative state of mind. This is not unlike the common-sense knowledge that, faced with a crisis, some of us panic and some of us become pillars of strength, displaying courage we didn't know was there. Certainly, the state of cognitive dissonance is, above all, one of motivation to act. Some writers have theorised that the tendency is to act towards reducing the dissonance, and indeed to avoid future dissonance or conflict (eg. Festinger, 1957). Halmos' view, on the other hand, is that instead of striving to eliminate dissonance, the counsellor retains it and that it is a desirable state of mind for the counsellor. He states:

> . . . the elements of the faith of the counsellors have one significant structural characteristic in common: they all affirm paradoxes. I believe that this affirmation is a psychological prerequisite to their performance, for it generates creative works and excites dedication and faith. (Halmos, 1965)

Halmos in fact advocates that there is a correlation between 'sanity' and the acceptance of dissonance. The capacity to tolerate, and indeed to thrive in an environment of uncertainty, ambiguity, paradox, and conflict would seem to be important for the helping professionals. The existence of such characteristics in the helping enterprise is well established - one can but hope that one is to some degree endowed with the Faith, or the Divine Providence, or the Inspiration, or whatever it is that one clearly needs to qualify not only as a helper, but a sane one to boot!

The helper is arguably the most important ingredient within the helping situation, and hence the emphasis in this chapter on some of the aspects of the helper which we believe are important. The only tool that helpers have to assist their clients is themselves. The dynamic use of self can only spring from an understanding of what the self is - of what we are as individuals, and our acceptance of this, and the ambiguities and paradoxes of living. Helpers ought to be growing and developing as individuals; involved as it were in an eternal struggle for self-knowledge and good mental health, in touch with reality, with the realness of themselves as individuals living in a social environment, and aware of their limitations, strengths and weaknesses.

4.10   Who is the You Nobody Knows?

Who is the you nobody knows
The private you who never shows
The you inside
The you you hide
From public view?

You're insubstantial light and shade
A wisp of mist
A doll parade
Your laughing eyes
A clever guise
To mask the pain

You buried deep in hurt and fright
A fragile you away from sight
Where lies your truth
Your anguished youth
Your silent tears

Unfold your petals
Reach for stars
The warmth of love
Can heal your scars
And you will find
Some people mind
Some people care

You're holding close in tight embrace
An inner you you will not face
Try letting go
And start to show
Just who you are

If you can't risk
What will you do?
But live alone
Inside of you
Inside the you nobody knows
The private you who never shows. (Krause, 1976)

62

CHAPTER FIVE

Communication

5.1 Overview

This chapter explores aspects of the process of communication, an understanding of which we believe to be absolutely crucial for effective helping. The point is made, first of all, that all behaviour has message potential, and consequently, it must be recognised that communication takes place at a variety of levels, both verbally and non-verbally.

Secondly, a model of the communication process is outlined. This serves a number of purposes. It will provide a framework for examining more closely some of the elements inherent in the process which, hopefully, will aid our understanding of how communication breaks down.

In our view, effective communication is a prerequisite for effective relationships. Many of our clients suffer from the impact of poor communication in their relationships with significant others. Our helping, then, has to be characterised by a quality of communication which may be somewhat foreign to our clients. (Note, that this may increase the anxiety level in our clients!)

Communication between helper and client is essentially a process of creating shared meaning, and hence, how each in the encounter perceives the other is crucial. The chapter concludes with a brief discussion of the nature of perception, and its role in the creation of meaning.

5.2 Communication and Communication Skills

Watzlawick and his associates believe that there is a property of behaviour that could hardly be more basic, and it is that behaviour has no opposite. In other words, there is no such thing as non-behaviour. One cannot not behave, though of course we can all mis-behave. But, even mis-behaving is behaving! This capacity not to not behave has implications in the interactional situations, where people are in face to face contact.

There is another property of behaviour that is often overlooked. That is, behaviour has message value. When we behave, we are sending messages, whether we like it or not. And whilst we believe we are communicating with specific, targetted individuals, we are in fact broadcasting messages to the world in general. In other words, our behaviour is a communication.

If we recognise the impossibility of not behaving, and couple this with the idea that behaviour has message value then, from this analysis, there are implications for interactional situations:

a. It follows then that no matter how an individual may try, he cannot not communicate. Activity or inactivity; words or silence; all have message value.

b. These messages or communications influence other individuals. These other individuals, in their turn, cannot not respond to these communications. As they, therefore, are themselves communicating, others cannot not, in their turn, again, not not respond! Communication is reciprocal and recursive.

c. Neither can we say that communication only takes place when it is intentional, conscious or successful, in the sense that mutual understanding takes place.

The impossibility of not communicating is a phenomenon of more than theoretical interest. It underpins the whole of the caring professions which, as part of the 'treatment', use words, and person-to-person contact. It undergirds the whole sphere of interpersonal relationships. Faulty communication, in the sense of being unsuccessful, is, we believe, at the root of most conflicts, whether these be between siblings in the same family, between spouses, between unions and management, or even between nations.

Because it is impossible not to behave and not to communicate, Watzlawick et al. (1967) draw attention to the schizophrenic, who for instance, is faced with the impossible task of denying that he is communicating, and at the same time denying that his denial is a communication. The schizophrenic dilemma of trying not to communicate, and yet, where even nonsense, silence, postural immobility, or any other form of denial is a communication, is somewhat similar to that of many of our clients and our relationship to them. It means that in our interaction with clients and others, we have to take cognisance of all behaviour, for all behaviour has message value.

Normally, we are pretty adept at 'reading' the other person, and communication is more or less successful, in the sense that a basic understanding or mutuality is obtained. This suggests that our communications (or behaviours) have to be consistent, congruent and accurate or else we add to the confusion of the client or patient. In our opinion lack of consistency in helpers is tantamount to a criminal offence, for we have no right whatsoever to add to the confusion of those already in difficulty.

The difficulty may be overcome if we recognise that behaviour, both verbal and non-verbal has message value. When we say something (verbal behaviour) it is usually accompanied by a number of non-verbal components. A statement can be made seriously, humorously, menacingly, casually, and so on. Voice tonal qualities also convey information, messages, eg. warmth or harshness. Similarly, the speed of delivery may tell us something about the content of the message, as well as something about the person delivering the message. Gestures, shrugs, facial grimaces all tend to add richness to verbal content.

These non-verbal components of the communication may act as modifiers of the verbal content. The tragedy of the double bind, for example, is that the 'I love you' verbal message is accompanied by non-verbal messages of hate or rejection. This kind of double message may be conveyed within verbal communication, or by offering radically inconsistent - perhaps even directly opposing - verbal and non-verbal communication.

The following extract was quoted by Paul Watzlawick (1974), as an example of the power and the destructiveness of the double-bind form of communicating. The extract is from 'Mary Poppins' by Pamela L. Travers:

'. . . 'I suppose, my dear' - she turned to Mary Poppins, whom she appeared to know very well - 'I suppose you've come for some gingerbread?'

'That's right, Mrs. Corry,' said Mary Poppins politely.

'Good. Have Fannie and Annie given you any?' She looked at Jane and Michael as she said this.

'No, Mother,' said Fannie meekly.

'We were just going to, Mother-' began Miss Annie in a frightened whisper.

At that Mrs. Corry drew herself up to her full height and regarded her gigantic daughters furiously. Then she said in a soft, fierce, terrifying voice: 'Just going to? Oh, indeed! That is very interesting. And who, may I ask, Annie, gave you permission to give away my gingerbread?'

'Nobody, Mother. And I didn't give it away. I only thought - '

'You only thought! That is very kind of you. But I will thank you not to think. I can do all the thinking that is necessary here!' said Mrs. Corry in her soft, terrible voice. Then she burst into a harsh cackle of laughter. 'Look at her! Just look at her! Cowardy-custard! Crybaby!' she shrieked, pointing her knotty finger at her daughter.

Jane and Michael turned and saw a large tear coursing down Miss Annie's huge, sad face, and they did not like to say anything, for, in spite of her tininess, Mrs. Corry made them feel rather small and frightened.'

Within half a minute, Mrs Corry has managed to block poor Annie in all three areas of human functioning: acting, thinking and feeling. She first implies that to give the children some gingerbread would have been the right thing to do. When her daughters are about to apologise for not having done this yet, she suddenly denies their right to take that action. Annie tries to defend herself by pointing out that she did not actually do it, but only thought of doing it. Mrs. Corry promptly lets her know that she is not supposed to think. The way the mother expresses her displeasure leaves no doubt that this is an important matter and her daughter had better be sorry about what happened. With this she manages to drive Annie to tears and then immediately ridicules her feelings. (Watzlawick, 1974)

In this extract, Mrs. Corry is described as using non-verbal behaviour - body language - which is entirely consistent with her overall threatening verbal communication. It is the antinomies in her logic which constitute the double- bind message. In other cases, mutually contradictory messages may be sent using both verbal and non verbal means simultaneously.

5.3 The Importance of Body Language
The extent of congruence between verbal and non-verbal communication is a particularly critical guide to determining the messages sent and

received by people. We won't attempt, here, to describe the many gestures and postures which people may adopt and what they may mean - there is already adequate coverage of this kind of information in the literature. We will, however, give consideration to some more general points to do with this important topic in communication.

Allan Pease has noted, in summarising much of the literature on body language, that most researchers agree with the notion that verbal communication is used mainly for conveying information, while non-verbal communication is used for:

> . . . negotiating interpersonal attitudes, and in some cases is
> used as a substitute for verbal messages. (Pease, 1981)

It is possible, then, to send greatly differing verbal and non-verbal messages simultaneously. This incongruence between the verbal and non-verbal elements within a message creates ambiguity and can make the message extremely difficult to interpret. There is a possibility, therefore, that whatever the interpretation made by a receiver of the message, it could well be wrong. Thus, leaving the sender of the message in the position of power in being able to accept or deny at will the other's interpretation of the message. We may or may not be aware, as senders, that we are doing this.

Allan Pease argues that non-verbal signals carry much more impact than verbal signals. Further, when the two are incongruent, there is a tendency for people to rely more on the non-verbal component of the message. As helpers, we have to ensure that we model congruence: that is, our verbal communication and our body language convey basically the same message. This is needed not only to achieve openness with our clients, and to facilitate a trusting relationship, but it also represents a demonstration of the kind of unambiguous communication which we would hope to encourage from clients.

As non-verbal communication most often conveys underlying attitudes, and also tends to be the communication channel with the most impact, helpers need to be especially sensitive to body language: both their own as well as that of the client.

Observing body language is not simply a matter of checking a list of items such as hand positions, eye contact, leg or arm movements and postures. It involves reading clusters of gestures and mannerisms in order to perceive the intended message. Pease talks about gesture clusters as though they comprise a 'sentence', any one word of which may have different meanings in another context or if taken alone:

> . . . scratching the head can mean a number of things -
> dandruff, fleas, sweating, uncertainty, forgetfulness. . .
> depending on the other gestures that occur at the same time.
> (Pease, 1981)

People with physical and/or intellectual disabilities may be unable to use certain gestures, and their body language may, therefore, be more difficult to read. This may create communication barriers for them even though their verbal communication may be unimpaired by the disability. As helpers, we should be aware of contingencies such as these, especially in the case of people who are temporarily disabled - they may experience increased frustration because their full ability to communicate has been disrupted. If the disability is temporary, they may not develop alternative or compensatory non-verbal routines, and so a significant part of their communication mechanism is unavailable to them.

It may be important to comment to clients upon the inconsistencies (as well as the consistencies) between their verbal and non-verbal signals. Equally, as helpers, it is useful if congruent communication is reinforced, because growing congruence in communication may be an indication of a movement towards a more 'healthy' relationship with the world.

We believe that this congruence is a reflection of self-understanding, and willingness to take responsibility (control) for one's own actions. As has already been highlighted, we consider these characteristics desirable.

5.4   The Communication Process
The communication process can be looked at from another point of view. Weaver (1967) reduced the complexity of the process to a few basic elements as outlined in the both in the two diagrammatic examples (p.69 and Appendix B) and in the following:

1. **The information source:** is the person who intends a message to be sent, (may or may not also be the transmitter of the message).

2. **The transmitter:** is the person who actually sends the message.

3. **Channel:** is the medium by which the message is sent.

4. **Receiver:** is the person who receives the message, (may or may not be also be the person for whom the message is destined).

A Model of the Communication Process

Weaver — 1967

Example 1.

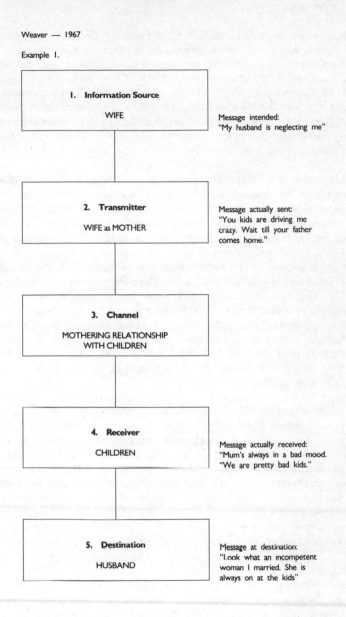

1. Information Source

WIFE

Message intended:
"My husband is neglecting me"

2. Transmitter

WIFE as MOTHER

Message actually sent:
"You kids are driving me
crazy. Wait till your father
comes home."

3. Channel

MOTHERING RELATIONSHIP
WITH CHILDREN

4. Receiver

CHILDREN

Message actually received:
"Mum's always in a bad mood.
"We are pretty bad kids."

5. Destination

HUSBAND

Message at destination:
"Look what an incompetent
woman I married. She is
always on at the kids"

5. Destination: is the person for whom the message is intended.

Let's consider a simple example of the use of the above terminology, within the frame of reference offered by Weaver. A newly married young woman, Barbara, is experiencing some disenchantment with her equally young husband, John, after only one year of marriage. As a couple they have had to negotiate few problems, but have developed no established pattern for dealing with conflict. Barbara complains, in a relatively understated way, to her Mother-in-law about John's behaviour and some of the difficulties she is experiencing. She also explains her diffidence about confronting John directly.

In this case, the information source is Barbara. She is also the transmitter. The channel used is the in-law relationship. The couple's relatively newly formed relationship is probably delicately balanced and, based until now, on a positive liking (mutual) and a desire of the parties to get on well with one another . . . at least at an overt level.

The mother-in-law is the receiver of the message, but the destination really intended is the husband, John. Barbara intends mother-in-law to pass on the message along with some 'good advice' to John. This effectively enables Barbara to side-step direct conflict with John. Since it is the avoidance of possible conflict which seems to bother Barbara, this 'plan', or communication game she has set in motion is designed to that end. It is of interest to note, at this point, that a helper working with this young woman may try to facilitate Barbara's skills in handling face-to-face conflict.

How might this particular communication process go awry? Let's think about one possible scenario, although there are probably many. Barbara may have miscalculated the mother-in-law's support for her. The mother-in-law may believe that Barbara's complaints are unjustified and are in fact an insult to her son and, indirectly, to herself. In this case, the message Barbara intended to send was definitely not the one (received and) interpreted by the mother-in-law. As a result, the message passed on to John by his Mother is not the one Barbara intended. What the mother-in-law passes on to her son is a warning about his nagging wife who is complaining about him behind his back!

What does John make of all this? John may surmise that there is some discord - rivalry, even - between his new wife and his Mother. He may decide this on the grounds that his wife has said nothing directly to him about being discontent with the marriage relationship. Based on his perception of the state of affairs, John may decide to take action to smooth over the ruffled relationship between the two women. Attending to problems in his marriage may not occur to him because he has received no clear message about them. He attributes his wife's discontentment (if any is apparent to him) to the problematic relationship she has with his mother!

One of the actions John may take is to pay a little more attention to his mother. Barbara would perceive this, and become even more discontent. Her plan, or communication game has failed because her communication was misdirected and ineffective. Another consequence may be that the mother-in-law may gain more attention from her son but lose the trust of her new daughter-in-law.

Haley (1968) points out that an individual can negate or modify the effect of his communication by changing any or all of the elements in the communication model. For example:

a. I was drunk - a negation of the source - (therefore this person is not responsible for what was said or done).

b. But I didn't say that! - denial of the reported message.

c. And if I did, I certainly didn't mean that! - denial of the receiver, and destination of the message.

d. I wouldn't have said such a thing in those circumstances - denial of the social matrix.

It can be seen from the foregoing examples that denial can play a very significant role in our communication. Denying the message, the receiver, the destination, and indeed the social matrix are ways of disowning our communication - ways of implying that it is not our communication, but some other component in the situation, which is the problem. Barbara's mother-in-law failed to supply to John adequate or accurate information, in part because she misinterpreted Barbara's message in the first place. It could be added that the misinterpretation may have been based on, for example, the mother-in-law's biased faith in her son along with a belief that as a new wife Barbara had no right to complain. Hence, the mother-in-law's belief system played a part in her interpretation of the communication.

By examining, with our clients, the process of communication they have used in problem situations, it is often possible for distortions such as these to be uncovered. Using a frame of reference such as Weaver sets out can assist the helper to ask certain kinds of questions for the client to consider. A helper may ask Barbara, for instance, how she communicated her marital unhappiness to her husband. In re-telling the tale, Barbara may be helped to see that it was this indirect communication process which initiated the downward spiral of distorted messages which resulted in John's spending more time with his mother just at the time when the marriage was in need of his efforts. It is one way of the helper developing a dialogue with Barbara about what messages she has sent to whom, and how they were picked up - it may facilitate Barbara's improving her communication skills in the future.

Distortions in communication can create more distortions - the spiralling effect of misperception built on misperception, with the protagonists reacting to messages which become further distorted with each reaction. At its worst, the process can become so entrenched that the parties are no longer able to untangle the messages at all. It is often at this point that professional helpers meet clients. Untangling the communication processes, using a frame of reference such as is exemplified here, can become a goal of the helping relationship, with helper and client collaborating to discover where the distortions have occurred, and why they have occurred.

So far we have used examples of ineffective or distorted communication. But there are plenty of examples of effective communication, and most of us engage in effective communication a good deal of the time. Effective communication which delivers the intended message, to the intended target, at the intended time and place, is just as useful to examine in the process of understanding communication. Indeed, as helpers we should always be ready to highlight, through feedback, those instances in which our clients have communicated effectively, as well as those in which they have not.

We have used, below, a delightful extract from the work of English novelist, Virginia Woolf, well-renowned for her skill in capturing the nuances of human interaction, to highlight an instance of extremely effective communication which was not at all direct. It is worth pondering over:

> An exquisite scent of olives and oil and juice rose from the great brown dish as Marthe, with a little flourish, took the cover off. The cook had spent three days over that dish. And she must take great care, Mrs Ramsay thought, diving into the soft mass, to choose a specially tender piece for William Bankes. And she peered into the dish, with its shiny walls and its confusion of savoury brown and yellow meats, and its bay leaves, and its wine and thought: This will celebrate the

occasion. . .

'It is a triumph,' said Mr Bankes, laying his knife down for a moment. He had eaten attentively. It was rich, it was tender. It was perfectly cooked. How did she manage these things in the depths of the country? he asked her. She was a wonderful woman. All his love all his reverence had returned; and she knew it.

'It is a French recipe of my grandmother's,' said Mrs Ramsay, speaking with a ring of great pleasure in her voice. (Virginia Woolf, To The Lighthouse)

5.5 Perception in Interviews
An important determinant of the quality of communication in any interaction situation is the perception each brings into the encounter, not only of each other, but also of the purposes of the interview as well as of the roles played by each participant.

Perception is essentially a construction: a constructive process through which meaning is attached to the myriad of stimuli which constantly bombard the individual. Kahneman (1973) suggests that individuals are active in determining which of the stimuli in the environment they will allow to control their behaviour. In other words, at an almost subliminal level, an individual in scanning the environment, chooses which stimuli he will attend to, or take notice of. Having made that 'decision', the chosen stimuli are then processed and meaning attached. Given exactly the same set of stimuli, it is unlikely that each member in a group of people will perceive the same picture, in exactly the same way. Furthermore, because of each individual's unique history, present, and hoped-for-future, the meaning attached to the picture will tend to be different for each member of the group.

The selective nature of attending means that the picture of reality created by the individual is thus, neither entirely accurate, nor entirely representative of the stimuli in the environment. Good and Brophy (1973), for example, indicate that on occasions, individuals think that they see reality (the world outside the individual) but in fact their biases, past experiences, and prejudices lead them to interpret what they see and this may or may not be congruent with reality. Research has shown that perception can be modified by conversion processes (Becker, 1963); group pressure (Asch, 1952; Sherif, 1936); by significant others (Epstein and Koromita, 1966); through ecological demands (Berry, 1972); and so on.

What we see, and what we respond to at any particular time, is a function of our 'internal conditions' (moods, anxieties, expectations and the like), and external features of the stimulus - shape, colour, movement, etc., and if this is another individual or group of people - by the sex, ethnic group, academic performance, personality, and so on.

This means that helpers must continually check their perception of themselves, their perceptions of the client, and their perceptions of what is happening in the interview. Our failure to listen carefully to a client may be a function of the way we perceive the client. For example, if we have an abhorence of 'deviant hairstyles', how may we react when we are confronted by a client with a hairstyle which we consider 'off-beat'? It may be that as we associate this kind of hairdo with certain kinds of people, we may not hear things from our client which, if listened to, would dis-confirm our initial perceptions. The meaning we have constructed based on a hairstyle which is not congruent with our own values, or whatever, may be completely out of tune with 'reality'. Therefore, the message we have received from the client, via the hairstyle, we may misinterpret to the ultimate harm of the client.

Let us assume that in our minds we associate deviant hairstyles with people who are anti-social and a threat to society. As part of our job, we have to make reports on the suitability of individuals as adoptive parents, or foster parents. We may be unlikely to offer a child to a person with such a hairstyle, particularly, if there is another applicant for the same child, with a more conventional hairstyle. This might mean for example, that we might fail to hear or discount the fact that the person with the deviant hairstyle has been successfully involved in childcare, youth groups and the like for a long time, in preference for the person with the more conventional hairstyle with little experience in working with children. We may be more impressed by the fact that she has attended university, and has a science degree.

5.6   How Meanings are Constructed
There is another aspect to this idea of selectively attending in order to arrive at our perception of the world. This is related to the fact that we are rarely presented with the complete information needed to understand situations to which we have to respond in our daily lives. This is especially the case when we consider our interactions with others. Hence, we frequently 'sketch in' what we believe are the missing bits in order to make sense out of situations. We use our past experience, and our innate tendencies to respond in certain ways as the bases upon which to build in the missing bits. This 'sketching in' process is undertaken because we generally prefer order to chaos, sense to nonsense - that is, we usually prefer to understand and make sense out of the stimuli

impinging upon us.

We have included examples of items from two tests in which perception plays a crucial role (p. 76). The first is the Gestalt Completion Test. The person completing the test has to fill in the spaces, as it were, to come to a decision about what the line-drawings represent. To complete the test, the individual has to have some idea, in his head, initially of the same or similar objects. Therefore, in a very real sense, he is having to call upon his background and his experience in order to complete the pictures. If for example, there was an incomplete drawing of a TV set, this would be meaningless to a Kalahari Bushman, who may never have seen a TV set.

The second example of a test involving perception is the Hidden Figures Test, in which an individual has to find a figure which is hidden or masked by a more complex figure. The person to complete this test accurately has to demonstrate 'analytical' skills, the ability to zero in and focus on the task, and to disregard extraneous stimuli. Many social workers and those in the caring professions tend to do relatively well on the Gestalt Completion Test, and relatively poorly on the Hidden Figures Test. The assumption is that these two tests measure ways in which individuals characteristically process stimuli from the environment. Helpers are continually in situations where they do not have all the information, where they have to sketch in the total picture, based on incomplete information.

In regard to the question of communication between individuals, Lyman and Scott (1970) have used a game framework to see how we order action and stimuli in social encounters. One basic proposition in the game framework is that:

> . . . all social games proceed from a condition of Imperfect Information. In this sense, every game includes an information game in which each player seeks to uncover the real identity, the actual intentions, and the secret strategems employed by the other. The condition of imperfect information renders all social games problematic. (Lyman and Scott, 1970)

To use Lyman and Scott's terminology, there is always an 'information game' in helping interviews, as well as in social encounters. An important outcome of the imperfect information idea is the recognition that the meaning arrived at by the individual, looking at his own behaviour and that of others, is partly comprised of 'made-up' information. This made-up information - like a story - consists of conclusions drawn about the present situation based on the individual's own past experiences and, of course, unique perception. It is not present or available from the present

Figure 5.2: Gestalt Completion Test Sample Items

Your task in this exercise is to fill in the gaps to complete the picture. There are spaces below for you to write in your answer!

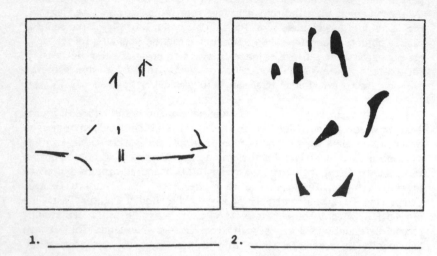

1. _____ 2. _____

Figure 5.3: Hidden Figures Test Sample Items

Your task in this exercise is to identify which one of the five shapes (A - E) is present in patterns 1, 2, 3. The shape to be identified in the pattern is exactly the same dimensions and direction as portrayed.

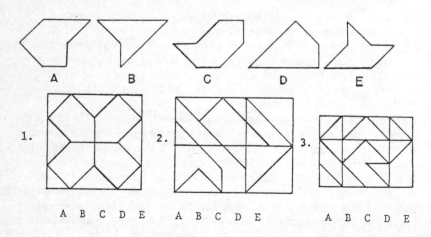

situation as stimuli. Since no two individuals share identical histories, the made-up component varies from person to person. Hence, the meaning, or interpretation placed upon situations or interactions differs from person to person. **The Sociology of the Absurd** (Lyman and Scott, 1970) uses the terminology 'constructing and reconstructing' social realities to describe this process of attaching meaning.

Distortions of reality or of communications between people, as well as misinterpretations and misunderstandings, often occur because the made-up component is a far cry from reality or from what was intended. In our work with clients, it is crucial to tease out the made-up component in their perception of what is happening to them, to discover the bases upon which that made-up component was constructed and its relation to the actual situation they are trying to deal with. Furthermore, we must be aware that, as helpers, we also 'create' made-up information in relation to how we perceive our client and the story they are trying to tell us. We have to continually 'perception check', a check of our understanding of what it is that we are being told.

Ellis (1973) in his Rational Emotive Therapy argues, inter alia, that the 'facts' of a situation are frequently distorted by the individual in such a way that the individual consequently makes a judgement about himself. For example, a person may not attempt to make a speech in public, a client may choose to avoid the risk of change, because of the possibility of failure, of not being good enough. The failure, or possible failure to act, is because the individual believes that a lack of success would make him a 'bad' person. The individual 'catastrophises' the possible outcomes, and as a result leaves himself paralysed.

Ellis is concerned about the ways in which individuals perceive and talk to themselves. He believes that in talking to ourselves, we frequently indoctrinate ourselves with distorted messages about our self worth. "If I don't do this well, it would be terrible, and I will therefore be a 'nogoodnick'."

The communication process is based on behaviour that is perceived, and interpreted, which in turn 'provokes' a response, which in its turn is responded to and so on. Communication not only occurs in overt interactional situations, ie. with other people, but also in dialogue with the self.

This chapter has raised some of the key concerns in our communication as individuals and as helpers. Of particular importance is the notion of congruence between verbal and non-verbal behaviour on our part, and on the part of clients. We have stressed the value in identifying discrepancies or misinterpretations in the communication that individuals have with one another.

We need to constantly check our perceptions of other people and events, and to ensure that as far as possible our communications both verbal and non-verbal accurately reflect what we feel, and that the messages picked by others in the interaction are what we intended to convey. The quality of our communication with our clients is, to a large extent, a determiner of the potential quality of the helping relationship that can be created with them.

CHAPTER SIX

Building and Developing the Relationship

6.1 Overview

In this chapter you will be introduced to some of the skills areas which we believe may be helpful in building up the kind of relationship which many of our clients need. The emphasis on skills areas is an attempt on our part to move away from the current emphasis on the teaching of skills (eg. Carkhuff, 1969; Ivey and Authier, 1978). Whilst we do not eschew the teaching of skills, it appears to us that, in many cases, these amount to little more than the mere learning by rote of mechanical responses to client statements. Our belief is that this 'recipe-book' approach to many client problems and difficulties may deny the dignity, competence and autonomy of our clients. Skills have to reflect caring values and attitudes; have to be natural and authentic and must not be limited by the parameters of any training programme.

It could well be argued, of course, that skills-training has to be a priority, for then this gives confidence to the helper. It is hoped that this confidence will flow into more 'authentic' helping (Brammer and Shostrum, 1977). Our experience has tended to show, however, that the shift from 'becoming' to 'being' a counsellor takes a considerable amount of time (MacLean, 1980) and that there is a strong possibility that trained incapacity functions to limit the effectiveness of many counsellors.

The notion of 'skills areas' also highlights the fact that skills, and the various components of more global skills, ought not to be learned in isolation. The plain fact of the matter is that in our professional practice as helpers we do not use components of skills, or the skills alone!

In our striving for self-conscious helping, the helper has to be able to indicate the reasons for his behaviour within the helping relationship. Furthermore, he ought to be able to indicate why it was that this strategy, skill or whatever was utilised and why other alternative behaviours were either not considered, or considered and rejected, in working with this unique client. Some of these issues will be addressed in this chapter.

6.2   Beginnings

The kind of helping that we are focusing upon in this book occurs through the encounter between two or more people in a context called an interview. Some helpers have labels attached to them - for example, counsellor, therapist, social worker, psychologist, psychiatrist and so on. Sometimes these labels are indicative of the characteristic ways the helper will intervene or describe the domain in which the helper feels comfortable. As psychiatrists are medically trained initially, they tend to feel more at home in medical settings, and in fact many of them utilise drugs and other medical interventions, in addition to 'talking', in assisting their clients (who tend to be called patients!)

The inter-personal contact occurs within specific parameters or sets of rules which outline the expected behaviours of both parties. Many of these rules are covert and are intuitively adhered to. The fact that these rules operate may lead to 'hegemonic' domination of one party to the encounter over the other. Generally speaking, however, the client to be a client has to demonstrate client-type qualities, some of which have been explored in a previous chapter. Conversely, the helper has to demonstrate helper behaviours and qualities in order to be considered an 'adequate' helper by the client, the profession and the agency for which the helper works. Failure of one party or the other to demonstrate the appropriate behaviours and attitudes may result in a failure of the interview to 'get off the ground'.

The reason for this discussion is to suggest to you that over time a number of myths, frequently encased in 'rules', about helper (and client) behaviour have been generated and, whilst there may be evidence to support such myths, the overly strict adherence to some of these myths may be counter-productive.

Intentional, purposive helping suggests that the helper must be aware of what he is doing and why! In essence, helping depends to a very large extent on obtaining from the client, her story, told in her time and in her own way, in order that the information obtained by the worker can be converted into knowledge which, in turn, can be mobilised to assist the client in whatever way is deemed to be appropriate. So how do we get this information - the raw stuff of helping?

Our first task when meeting with a client is to put her at ease. The purpose is to allow her to relax as much as possible in order to get down to the business of identifying her issues and concerns as quickly as possible (Okun, 1976). There is, then, a purpose behind making the client feel comfortable, and that purpose is to get her into the business of the meeting as quickly as possible.

Many counsellors and social workers, unfortunately, spend an inordinate amount of time in making the client ostensibly feel at ease, with the frequent result that much time is spent discussing the weather (if you are English), the football (if an antipodean), or the garden! This degeneration into passing the time of day may be very comforting for both the client and the helper, in that they are colluding with each other to avoid making a contact which could be potentially painful to either or both of them. This is not to suggest that talking about the weather, football, the garden, the family or fishing may not be appropriate, provided that the helper can justify his behaviour and show that it was intentional!

In fact, many clients feel at ease if the counsellor or helper demonstrates a degree of expertness and an air of competence. There has been very little research into whether or not clients are helped more by being interviewed in surroundings which are comfortable and maybe plush, as against the more 'clinical' surroundings of a public service utility interview room! Many clients, in fact may feel discomfort at being interviewed in surroundings which are unfamiliar, whether this is because they are too comfortable or too utilitarian. Perhaps, though, the comfort of the worker is more important than that of the client!

A good way to start is to invite your client to tell you what has been going on or to ask the client how you can help them. These kinds of ice-breakers can help focus on the reason for the meeting. Ivey (1971) suggests that clients be given an 'open invitation to talk', usually by way of an 'open-ended question or statement'. An open-ended question or statement is any comment which attempts to preclude the possibility of a mono-syllabic reply; ie. 'yes' or 'no'. The skill of asking open-ended questions is somewhat difficult to acquire, but we have found that it is a very powerful technique in the acquisition of information.

Many workers seeking to obtain information about the client and her family may tend to ask specific or 'closed-type' questions, for example, 'How many children do you have?'; 'What are their ages?'; 'Which school do they go to?' and so on. Whereas an open-ended request such as 'Tell me about your family?' does two things. Firstly, it gives the helper that kind of overt information about the family which the client is prepared to disclose. Secondly, to the extent that the client has a choice about how much and about the nature of the information to disclose, it gives control of the information-flow to the client. The client is ostensibly in control. However, this control is somewhat illusory, because, as we learned from the last chapter, even silence is a communication, therefore, those things that the client has not told us about the family and so on, may be more meaningful than those things that the client has disclosed!

One of the writers, for example, was involved in a household survey investigating the patterns of contact between members of families and some of the processes of family life. One of the questions in the structured interview related to the number of children within the family. This was asked in an open-ended kind of way, and the interviewee talked at length about her three children. There were in fact, photographs of four children around the room. Over time, this discrepancy was delicately broached by the interviewer, and it transpired that one of the children was a 'hydrocephalic child' and that child's existence was more or less being denied by the mother. It had been placed in a psychopaedic hospital and, apparently, out of sight, meant out of mind!

During this particular phase, the quality of questioning is extremely important. It can quickly degenerate into what we call 'verbal ping-pong', where a closed question is followed by a closed reply, followed by a closed question and a closed reply in monotonous, and usually uninformative, exchanges between client and helper. Careful and skilful verbal behaviour has to be accompanied by a sensitive, caring 'looking'. Watch your client very carefully for signs of strain or stress, particularly in discussing significant others, and in skirting around or ignoring topics, events, people and so on. The non-verbal behaviour of your client, as was discussed in the previous chapter, may be a more important indicator of feelings, tensions and strains than his verbal behaviour. This kind of sensitivity is extremely important, particularly in the initial stages of contact with the client.

6.3 Attending Behaviours

In our everyday lives we are bombarded by stimuli to which we respond in a variety of ways. We process the information that impinges upon our senses, more or less automatically, and without too much conscious effort. Kahneman (1973) goes somewhat further than this and argues that we process at a 'deeper' level that stimulus material which we want to 'look' at again, in order to determine whether or not we really want to look at it. So what happens is that we construct a picture, and add meaning to it, and it is the meaning of the picture or stimulus that is given that determines whether or not we are in fact going to take any notice of the picture. There is a threshold which has to be breached, in order for us to take notice and, if appropriate, take action. The advertising media know this only too well, and attempt to breach this threshold by noise, colour, size, repetition as well as by persuasion. The typical television advertisement has these kinds of qualities, and our role, as a consumer, is to be acted upon, to be passive. If the advertising is quality advertising, we may indeed take notice of it. Much of the 'looking' at television involves a kind of active non-looking. We selectively attend to those things which are important for us, and tend to 'switch off' if what we are looking at is not important.

In helping, however, there are crucial differences. Our looking has to be active. Our looking involves searching for new information; processing that information at a deeper level. It also involves 'filling in the gaps'; trying to make sense of the information that we are being presented with by the client. It is an active process of creating meaning. The creation of meaning can present us with difficulties, in that our meaning may have to be shared with the client, or else we may be literally building sandcastles in the air! We need also to be aware of those things which we consider to be important that we are going to attend to at a deeper level. That is part of what is meant by being a self-conscious helper! Clearly the manner in which we attend to our clients is important.

Paying attention, however, has other dimensions. In watching television advertisements, our attention is being clamoured for, is being actively sought by the advertiser, who wishes you to do something as a result of watching the advertisement. In helping, the client should not have to compete for attention. It is being given freely. The reaction to this, is that clients tend to feel that they matter. Furthermore, paying close attention to your client indicates respect and a feeling that what she is saying is of value and importance, and that she is a person of worth.

There are a number of myths that surround the notion of paying attention and they need to be noted. First of all, not everything that our clients say is important. Obviously some things are more important than others, and we have to be aware of why it is that we are viewing some things as more important than others! Secondly, there may be occasions when it is a good idea not to pay attention to the client. Attention giving is rewarding for the 'attention-seeker'. Most counsellors differentially respond to their clients, rewarding them with their attention when the clients have been 'good'. In our book, the so-called 'non-directive' counsellors may not be 'self-conscious' counsellors because of the denial, implicit in their appellation, of selective attending and responding to clients. Counsellor attention giving can be a very powerful moulder of client behaviour. Therefore, we need to know, as self-conscious counsellors, just what it is that determines what is the 'good' that we want to 'reward' with our attention!

Fischer (1978) quotes research which suggests that the following aspects of attending behaviour contribute to effective helping:

A. Obtaining and maintaining good eye contact:
Look at your client but do not stare at her; make your eye contact natural - as natural as possible. Many counsellors and helpers have taken the dictum 'good eye contact is essential' to suggest that eye contact must be maintained at all times and under all conditions! Do not pin your client to her chair, like a transfigured butterfly, by insensitive, unrelenting eye-contact.

B. Maintaining a relaxed, natural comfortable posture:
This is an important aspect of attending behaviour. However, do not relax so much that you want to go to sleep! Do not insult your client by putting your feet on the desk, or other kinds of postures which indicate either that the client is of little worth and ought not to be taken seriously, or that you are not really interested in the client, and that you wish you were doing something else. If that is the case, then you ought to discuss this with the client. One of our former colleagues used to go to sleep whenever he had in for interview a certain client. The client used to bore him to death! In the end this was discussed with the client and a new worker was found.

C. Leaning slightly towards the client:
Fischer argues that this helps to build up contact between the helper and the client. If your client moves back in his chair, it could be that somehow you are intruding upon his personal space in some way, indicating a desire for a less intimate contact, and more space in which to move around.

Our observations of counsellors at work over a number of years suggests that this may become an unnatural stereotyped behaviour, with the result that its artificiality has an impact on the client - for the worse. There is no doubt, however, that when we want to confide we tend to move forward towards the person we are talking to and, if under threat we move away from the other person. Frequently in counselling, a major shift in the topic under discussion, new disclosures and so on are accompanied by major shifts in body posture. Sometimes these body movements presage a change of direction in the interview. Sometimes they are consequential. There is no doubt that marked shifts in body posture, the movement of chairs, any marked physical movement is a signal to the worker that a change has or is about to take place within the interview. Occasionally, the change occurs only within the client's head, and is immediately manifested in a change of topic or whatever, in the interview. It is a good idea to check this possibility out with your client. The helper has also to be aware of changes in his body posture, and their meaning.

D. Using appropriate and congruent facial expressions:
Many helpers, feeling the need to be loved and to be warm in their relationships, smile all the time, even when the client is relating that they are not feeling particularly happy. What occurs is an incongruence between the message given out by the client and the perceived effect this has on the helper. If helpers believe that it is important to be in touch with the kinds of things that the client is saying, then it is important to mirror this, to some extent in their expression.

E. Using relaxed, spontaneous head, arm and body movements:
Again, spontaneity is the key here. The client has to be assured that he is talking to a real person (or else how can he be real?). Too often in the past, the therapist was seen as a person devoid of feelings who maintained a stony face throughout the contact with the client. Social workers during the 1950's and 1960's were 'trained' to use their hands in a certain way, somewhat akin to a seal's flipper movement, as if offering encouragement to the client to keep talking. That together with the social worker's 'smile' mentioned above (the smile was somewhat reminiscent of Charles Dickens' Wemmick's 'post-office mouth'), created an artificiality and were frequently identifying characteristics of 'trained' social workers, manifested in all situations, professional and personal.

F. Listen carefully to what your client is saying:
It is important that you remember what you hear and, more importantly perhaps, remember how it was said. As helpers, we need to listen to our clients, and to hear what it is that they are saying and, as previously mentioned, hear what it is that they are not saying! If necessary, do not be afraid to make notes. Ask your client for permission; usually it will not cause any problem. Some helpers tape-record interviews, and after the first few minutes the presence of the tape-recorder is usually forgotten as the business of the interview progresses.

Your listening should be aided by your eyes. Look at the way your client tells her story; remember that communication operates on a number of different levels. Look to see how your client modifies her story by non-verbal means - shrugging of shoulders, expression in her voice, and the clearing of the throat. Non-verbal cues enrich the spoken word and add feelings to the content of what is said.

6.4 Minimal Encouragers
The task of the helper is to get the client to 'tell her story in her own particular way, at her own pace in her own time'. The utilisation of open-

ended questions, statements or comments gives the client permission to talk about the things that are important to her. Once a client begins to tell you her story, the initial task is to keep her talking. Client talk is the data we need in order to begin to understand what it is that is bothering the client, how she perceives her world and the meaning that this has for her. To maintain client talk we use techniques which come under the heading of 'minimal encouragers'. These are the little words like 'yes', 'go on', 'tell me more', 'so?', 'oh', and so on which function to let the client know that the focus of the interview is still on her; that you are tuned in to her and want her to continue. They let the client know that you are participating in the interview, are actively involved, but not wanting to interfere or detract from what she is trying to say. In the initial stages of any contact with a client, the ratio of client talk to helper talk must be in favour of the client.

One of our counsellor trainees was working in a school situation with a teenage boy. The boy was so good at using minimal encouragers that in a transcript of the interview, out of 220 lines of dialogue, he contributed about 10%, and this largely consisted of minimal encouragers. The trainee counsellor had lost control of the interview process and was being effectively counselled by the teenager who was supposed to be the subject of the counselling process! The intriguing aspect of this, and a sad commentary at that, was that the counsellor trainee was not aware that this was happening.

At the end of the counselling session, the trainee proclaimed that he had done a good job of counselling the boy. In this trainee's mind was the equation of counsellor talk with good counselling. More often than not the opposite is in fact the case. The quality of the counselling is a function of the quality of the listening, primarily. If the helper is talking, there is no way in which he can be listening!

Other minimal encouragers include 'huh huh' and 'head nodding'. The head nodding is not of the kind used by television reporters in television interviews. Frequently, television interviewers will nod vigorously at the interviewee, and you wonder whether it is in response to a direction printed on a flash card telling them to 'nod encouragingly'. The result is often quite bizzare. On the other hand, you will find that good counsellors tend to nod their heads most of the time. They tend to use very fine head movements which are not intrusive, but which tend to operate almost at the subliminal level. They are, however, quite effective in keeping the client talking!

The problem at times may be the reverse. It may be difficult to stop your client from talking. This can be achieved by direct intervention in the sense that you take overt control once again of the interview. Alternatively, you can achieve this indirectly by not reinforcing the client's talking, for example, by reducing and maybe eliminating eye contact, and by the strategic non-use of minimal encouragers!

6.5 Perception Checking

'Perception checking' relates to a family of skills which is primarily concerned with the helper's attempts to understand as fully as possible the story the client is telling. These skills have the dual function of keeping the helper on the right track, and again letting the client know that you are really trying to be with them. It is easy for helpers to fall into the trap of beginning to imagine what is wrong with the client or, because of their own past experiences, perhaps, to identify with what they believe the client's difficulties to be.

Helpers may, then, begin to insert their ideas and fantasies into their client's story, thus subtly distorting the story. This can be further compounded when a helper, after making a judgement as to what is wrong, starts to move the client into treatment areas based on his misperceptions of the client's story. Perception checking is essential for all helpers, and must continue all the way through the contact with the client.

The following are some of the ways in which perception checking can be undertaken:

1. Clarification: if you are not sure that you have heard your client correctly, you may ask her to repeat herself; or you may ask her to elaborate a point that she has made, in order that you may have that part of her story clarified. Do not be afraid to admit to yourself, if not to your client that you are somewhat confused about the wealth of data being presented to you. It is preferable that you use open ended questions, because you do not want to get into the question and answer game of verbal ping-pong! Remember also that clarification may be confronting, or the word we prefer - challenging, to the client, particularly if the clarification concerns an apparent discrepancy within her story. The point being made here is that, if your client is somewhat defensive, and you are seeking clarification, it ought to be a professional judgement about how the clarification is sought.

2. Summarisation: is another means of perception checking. The helper attempts to summarise where he believes the client is at, and gets feedback from the client in terms of the veridicality of the helper's perceptions. In this case, the helper is seeking the help of the client in obtaining a more accurate picture of the client. This means that the helper should be solicitous, and non-blaming for his not fully understanding what it is the client is trying to say. In other words, it is not the client's fault if the helper does not understand; it is the responsibility of the helper to understand as fully as is possible the story being told, and hence, it is the helper who must seek to clarify, and to summarise that which has been heard.

Summarisation is also used as a means of slowing down the communication process within the interview, and helpers frequently use this skill as a means of giving them some breathing space. It allows the helper to express aloud what he has grasped of the client's story to date. Do not be upset, if the client says 'NO! that's not correct', because this provides you with the opportunity to obtain the clarification required. It may also incidently give you an indication of the nature of the relationship between you and your client. Generally speaking, if a client feels sufficiently safe to correct you, this could be taken as an indication that the relationship is developing along the right lines.

Summarisation, together with the other skills in this area - paraphrasing and reflecting - function to give feedback to the client about the way she is 'coming across' to the helper. This is frequently a new experience for the client. It gives her a chance, when in a safe environment, to listen to how she sounds and how she is perceived by others. We have had clients say to us 'Is that really how I sound?'; 'Is it really as bad as that?', thus, prompting them to think about their concerns at a somewhat deeper level. Furthermore, accurate feedback helps the movement of material into the area of 'open-activity' in the Johari model of the helping process.

3. Paraphrasing: this important skill is much used by beginning helpers, very badly, and it often degenerates into 'parrot-phrasing'. Paraphrasing is a skill which allows you to check what your client is saying. In a very real sense, this skill is concerned with letting the client know that you can understand the content of the message that she is communicating. Beginning helpers and counsellors tend to paraphrase the client's every statement - this is not necessary. In fact, unless used wisely and judiciously, this particular skill can slow down the whole interview process, and effectively prevent the client working on his problem. This is because every statement is said twice! It could be of course, that the client and counsellor have entered into some collusion to prevent any real work being done. This will always need to be watched.

4. Reflecting: is a very important clarification and perception checking skill. It is very difficult to learn, and to use correctly. Reflecting is an attempt to show the client that you subjectively understand the situation and her feeling or experiencing of that situation, or at least you are making that attempt. Reflecting in essence, is a paraphrase of the 'feelings' content of a client's statement. It differs from paraphrasing in that paraphrasing makes no real attempt to identify for the client (and of course, the helper too) the feelings implicit within the statement just made by the client.

Beginning helpers frequently fall into the trap of believing that if they preface any response to a client with the words 'You feel. . .' that they are using the skill of reflecting. This may not be so. So often these words preface psuedo-paraphrasing, and are merely words! This will be discussed in more detail below.

5. Confrontation: is a skill which should be rarely used by embryonic helpers. Confrontation is a perception checking skill in that the helper has, perhaps, noted a discrepancy in the client's story, or a discrepancy between the client's verbal and non-verbal behaviour, and is seeking a resolution or explanation of the discrepancy. Confrontation does have its dangers, as will be shown in the next section.

6.6   Responding for What?
It becomes obvious from the brief description of the skills discussed above, that the helper is, or ought to be, responding for a purpose! So many helpers fail to realise that their responses are supposed to have a purpose and, accordingly that they are intentional behaviours within the interaction between them and their client. The quality of the responding in a helping situation demonstrates the expertise of the helper, and whether or not he is working in the relationship for the benefit of the client. A number of the skills are utilised primarily to encourage the client to tell her story, and to continue telling it. Other skills focus on the building of rapport between the client and helper, and assist in the creation of a climate in which the client begins to feel safe and, perhaps, secure enough to start exploring where she is in relation to her problems. Reflection and confrontation skills open up new dimensions in the relationship in that these skills enable and facilitate the client to begin to do some work and to begin, perhaps, to really look at herself.

Empathy:
Reflecting is a crucial component of what is meant by 'empathy'. Once the feelings have been accurately understood, the next step is to accurately communicate that understanding to the client. Empathy, then, involves the communication of that understanding to the client. But, that is only the beginning of the so-called empathic process. For the process to develop even further, there must be some communication back from the client acknowledging the attempt to be empathic. There is little point in

attempting to be empathic, if the empathic attempts are not being picked up, or acknowledged by the client.

Reflecting requires not only the accurate perception of the content of the client's message, but also the manner in which it was said - the accurate perception of the non-verbal elements in the communication - and an accurate view of the feelings being expressed. This understanding is conveyed to the client by an appropriate verbal or non-verbal response of the helper.

> Mayeroff (1971), puts it this way - ' To care for another person, I must be able to understand him and his world as if I were inside it. I must be able to see, as it were, with his eyes what his world is like to him and how he sees himself. Instead of merely looking at him in a detached way from outside, as if he were a specimen, I must be able to be with him in his world, 'going' into his world in order to sense from 'inside' what life is like for him, what he is striving to be and what he requires to grow' (Egan, 1976).

Fischer (1978) points out that a common mistake of many clinicians, as noted by Fix and Haffke (1976), is to ask, when attempting to be empathic, 'How do you feel about that?' or 'How did that make you feel?' These questions would be asked no matter how obvious are the client's feelings. But the accurately empathic clinician would tend not to ask them since the rather awkward question, 'How do you feel?' indicates a low level of empathy, ie., an inability to observe what the client is communicating. Instead, the empathic worker would indicate by facial expression, tone of voice, and words a recognition of the client's feelings, or, at least, explore how he or she thinks the client might feel.

Additive Empathy:
Additive empathy goes further than empathy in that it adds an interpretive component. Additive empathy gets at not only what the other person states and expresses, but also what she implies, leaves unstated or does not clearly express (Egan, 1976). Egan also cautions that additive empathy should not be used too early in a relationship or in a group interaction, as it can be too frightening. It assumes that a relatively solid relationship has already been formed. It may according to Egan (1976), smack of 'psychologising', unless handled very well. As such, helpers may lose credibility with clients who, quite rightly, do not want to be 'psychologised'.

The following extract from an interview gives the flavour of empathy and additive empathy:

Girl   'Those kids are absolutely stupid; look at the way they behave. They are always in trouble.'

Helper A   'Those kids seem pretty stupid to you.' (Empathy).

Helper B   'Wouldn't it be nice if you could let your hair down like them, uh!' (Additive empathy)

In the examples above, there are qualitative differences between the responses of Helper A and Helper B. The interpretive component of the additive empathy response goes beyond the information given, and hence can be a very creative aspect of the relationship. It enables the client to face some of those hidden meanings, which may have been too uncomfortable to acknowledge previously.

But because of its interpretive nature, there is considerable room for error in the making of additive empathic responses by the helper. If the error element is too great, too frequent, or if the additive responses are inappropriately timed, measured in a sense by the amount of denial and correction from the client, then not only will you make the client angry, but any rapport that had been built up may be very quickly eroded.

The purpose of empathic and additive empathic responses should enable your client to look at herself, her experiences, strengths and weaknesses, her values and so on, in more depth. It could provide a new way of looking at herself, of gaining insight into attitudes, behaviours, etc. and the effect these are having on her difficulties, problems or concerns. It should enable the client to also express and own, hopefully, some of her deepest feelings, some of which she may not have been prepared to acknowledge until now. Empathic and additive empathic responses are really designed to make the client do some work - to look at herself. This work needs to be done in silence, or at least with minimal interruption from the helper. Helpers need to, therefore, allow the client time and space to 'work through' the effect of the empathic or additive empathic response. One counsellor-trainee made a very nice empathic response to a girl considering leaving college prematurely, but immediately followed it up with a question about her grades! She responded to the question about grades, and the opportunity for an exploration of where she was in relation to the empathic response, was lost. You will note the importance of giving clients time and space to reflect on empathic responses in the model to be outlined in the next section.

6.7   A Process Model of Empathic Understanding
Lyn Yeoman (1984) in her research into the nature of empathy, suggested on the basis of her literature review and empirical work, that there might

be eight phases in the empathic process. This is indicative of the fact that the notion of empathy is indeed complex. What tends to happen is that theorists and practitioners, she believes, in their attempts to measure empathy, tend to capture parts of the whole, and not the whole itself. She, therefore, believes that our understanding of what empathy is, always tends to be partial.

The first step in the process model she outlines comprises those pre-conditions which must exist before empathy can occur. The preconditions relate to the lower threshold for empathic potential. In other words, a helper to be empathic must first of all demonstrate a sensitivity to other people and to what is going on around him. This initial sensitivity 'tunes' the helper into where the client might be at, and what the client might be feeling. If the helper is tone deaf, to use a musical analogy, then there is little chance whatsover that the helper could ever be empathic. The helper in order to be empathic must possess at the very least, a modicum of attitudes, beliefs and philosophies which orient him to helping others. The preconditions are, then, largely comprised of those attitudes, values, skills and awarenesses which exist within the helper and which are, and have been, manifested in caring, compassion and so on for others, prior to any contact with the client.

Human beings have the capacity to tune into others' feelings, and to be moved by music, literature, film, drama, beauty. We have the capacity to identify with heroes, athletes and those whose feats, endurance, and skills we can admire. Most of us will respond with warmth to a small child putting their hand in ours, with a degree of distress to a small child in pain and so on. These responses to the human condition are part and parcel of the kind of thing Yeoman believes comprise the preconditions for empathic understanding. In essence, our capacity to respond appropriately, emotionally and to acknowledge these feelings within ourselves potentially make it possible for us to respond empathically.

Unfortunately, many of us, by our up-bringing and by the socialisation of the wider society have blunted our emotionality, and we find it difficult to tune into our own feelings, and to experience ourselves as we really are. If this has occurred within us, what tends to happen is that the empathic threshold has been raised to such an extent that we are unaware of the feelings being expressed by others, except when expressed in the grossest of ways.

In addition to being sensitive to the projected ambience of others through our awareness of ourselves, which assists in providing the preconditions for an empathic contact, Yeoman believes that an empathic contact is facilitated where there is a perceived similarity between the helper and the client. The perceived similarity exists more in terms of broad based similarities of values position, the recognition of having experienced similar emotions, being involved in similar activities, experiencing similar living conditions and so on. The emphasis is on broad based similarities. There is no need to have experienced the 'same' specific incidents, places, emotions or whatever. For example, helpers need not to have experienced death or divorce, but do need to have experienced loss, hurt, anger and other emotions which tend to underpin these more specific life events. The process of identification which comprises the second element in the Yeoman model, points to the 'unconscious' or 'out of awareness' recognition and acceptance by the helper of the other as worthy, as having inherent dignity as a human being. This 'pre-cognition' opens the way for the next step in the process.

Yeoman, calls the third element in her model 'incorporation', which she perceives as the 'reciprocal' of identification. By being aware of the dignity of the other, we are in effect re-affirming our own dignity. Thus, self-awareness leads to the possibility of being aware of others. Recognising and accepting ourselves as worthy, we are then able to believe in the 'worthiness' of our clients. In this element of the model, incorporation is concerned with the re-affirmation of those things which are viewed by the helper as being 'similar' in the client. So identification and incorporation are two sides of the same coin. Incorporation involves the active bringing of the client as a person into the very being of the helper. This is difficult to grasp but is concerned with, as it were, making room for the client, warts and all, within the helper. If there is a selectivity on the part of the helper, then acceptance (another useful concept here) of the client may be partial only. So if I believe that I, as a person am worthy, acceptable and so on, I am more likely to perceive these qualities as an integral part of the client. This identification then, reinforces my own worthiness and so on - incorporation.

These twin processes are somewhat akin to the Piagetian notions of assimilation and accommodation.

The propensity to respond in a caring way to clients, together with the processes of identification and incorporation lead to the next part of the model, where the helper gains new 'insights' into the person of the client. According to Yeoman, at this stage in the process, there is the possibility of a 'reverberation' between the rhythms of the client and the helper - a kind of resonance - in the encounter between the two. This point in the interview has a quality which sets it apart from the rest of the encounter. Good helpers can, with their clients, identify almost unerringly this particular point in the interview, even some considerable time after the closure of the interview. It represents a 'high point', where there was a closeness, an intimacy between the helper and the client. There is, in a sense, a recognition of the self in the other, by both parties, reminiscent of the 'I-Thou' encounter of Martin Buber.

The importance of the 'high point' in the encounter must not be over-emphasised because it is a precursor of work to be done by both the helper and the client. The danger for the helper (and as a result, for the client) is that the helper may want to continue or to maintain the 'high'. Failure to do so may cause the helper to feel that they have not been as effective as they might have been, and thus, there may be a pursuit of 'sharing' and intimacy by the helper at the expense of the client.

Yeoman quite rightly points out that the 'high' is followed by 'detachment'. Detachment is the cognitive accompaniment to the feelings content of the 'high'. It is the necessary withdrawal by the helper to ponder the meaning of the 'high', where the meaning of it is processed. This certainly fits in with our model of self-conscious helping. The reverberation does not have to be responded to immediately and, if it is, the response may be inappropriate. The need for the analysis of the experience - the 'I' and 'me' notion previously explored - points to the cognitive component of empathy. A component which seems to have been forgotten by many theorists and practitioners who focus almost exclusively on 'feelings'.

The sixth element in the empathic process, according to Yeoman, is the communication, in some way or other, of the felt awareness and insight into the other's experience. The timing of this is crucial in allowing for the impact of the possibly 'empathic moment' to be capitalised upon, for the benefit of the client! 'Responding for what?'- underlines the importance of this aspect for the helper. The purpose of the empathic moment is to allow the client to be able to more fully explore the meaning of their experience, part of which is the present encounter between the helper and client. So silence may be the most powerful response, at least initially to the 'high point' in the interview. Certainly, detachment suggests that the use of silence may well be appropriate, if not necessary. The empathic responding recipe-models of helper training to which we have alluded earlier, fail to recognise that the most appropriate response to the 'high' may take place very much later in the interview. Thus, the analysis of interview scripts for empathic responses to client statements may both inhibit and deny the presence of true empathic responses, particularly where they are of a non-verbal nature. Therefore, at some stage in the interview, the helper must make a decision, a professional judgement - the 'me' analysis of the 'I' - to communicate an acknowledgement of the empathic 'high' which was experienced by both helper and client. This communication by the helper, however conveyed, is a personal statement of the meaning of the 'high' for him. It is a personal statement, a very personal statement.

This personal statement is the end-point of the empathic process which has been largely the property of the helper. In the last two phases of the empathic process the focus shifts to the client. Unless the client makes a response, it is unlikely that the 'empathic circuit' has been closed or completed.

The client receives the message, and tries it out for 'goodness of fit'. If the client rejects the message, or denies the occurrence, then this may suggest that the timing of the communication is faulty, or that the quality of the relationship is such that it is not safe for the client to acknowledge the message, assuming that it was heard! Reception of the personal communication of the helper's personal message about the 'sharing' is, thus, the next stage in the empathic process. This phase of the empathic process requires a great deal of cognitive activity - thinking, reflecting, remembering and so on by the client. The helper must allow clients the time and silence to do some work. In this phase of the process, like the previous one, the temptation for helpers is to intervene too quickly, to talk too much and to break the silence needed by the client to explore at a much deeper level feelings, thoughts, memories and so on. If this occurs the potential of the empathic communication is lost.

The last element in the empathic process outlined by Yeoman (1984) occurs when the client gives some discernible feedback to the helper which indicates the degree of accuracy or otherwise of the communication or of the insight gained by the helper. Yeoman suggests that:

> The eight-phase model is presented as a way of understanding the link between the covert and the overt; the affective and the cognitive; the innate and learned components of empathy, each of which has been described by various theorists at some stage throughout history, as being the pre-eminent component of empathy. (Yeoman, 1984).

Yeoman's model pulls together a number of components which make up the empathic experience. By linking them together in this way, Yeoman is suggesting that the isolation of empathic components for analysis without due regard to other components is a recipe for not understanding the essence of empathy. Indeed, part of her argument is that the more the concept of empathy is analysed, the more likely its character will remain elusive.

The recognition, the acceptance of, and the our reflection upon our experience involves a great amount of cognitive activity. Our hearts and brains work hand in hand! The over-emphasis on feelings and 'letting it all hang out' needs to be counterbalanced, to give due recognition to the 'brainwork' required to process the 'feelings-work'.

The following poem was given to one of us, by one of our students. It is worthwhile noting that the poem captures a much larger sphere of human activity than feelings alone.

6.8   All of my Feelings are my Friends

My **ANGRY** feelings are there, to give me strength and conviction when I feel threatened or hurt.

My **FEAR** feelings are there to protect me in times of danger.

My **GUILTY** feelings are there to warn me when I might offend against my own beliefs.

My **AGGRESSIVE** feelings are there to give me courage and determination in overcoming obstacles.

My **TENDER** feelings are there to inspire me to care always for those in need.

My **SEX** feelings are there to give me joy in love and parenthood.

My **FAMILY** feelings are there to remind that I always want to belong.

My **FOOD** feelings are there to give me pleasure in partaking of my share of "our daily bread".

My feelings for **THINGS** are there to fulfil my need for privacy, comfort and security.

My **LEARNING** feelings are there to remind me that I will always desire to know and understand, and above all,

My **LOVE** feelings are there to guide and direct me in recognising, accepting and expressing my friendly feelings, in one, happy, harmonious WHOLE.

6.9 Confrontation

Confrontation, or the word we prefer, 'challenging', is a technique which should only be used by experienced counsellors. Challenging a client may make the client feel under threat or exposed and vulnerable. These are conditions which heighten anxiety in the client and may result in the client's responding with anger, tears, withdrawal, sometimes even depression. Egan (1976) suggests that confrontation is anything that you do which invites the client to examine her own behaviour and attitudes and their consequences a little more closely. He believes that confrontation if used skillfully by a caring person can serve the interests of both parties in the interpersonal transaction.

Simpson (1976) has set out some of the criteria which he believes ought to be used in considering whether or not the technique of confrontation or challenging should be used.

Considerations before using confrontation methods:
(a)   Recognise your own feelings. Is the statement you are going to make, more telling about you than the client? Is your reaction a reasonable reaction? Does it reveal subjective bias on your part - are you taking your hang-ups out on the client?

This is an essential part of self-conscious helping as defined in this book. You must be aware of what it is that is 'driving' you to want to challenge at this point in time in the interview. Why now, and why not at some other time? Just as timing is crucial in the empathic process, because of the challenging nature of the personal statement by the helper, it is also crucial when exploring some discrepancy or other in the client's story. Simpson also asks if self-disclosure on the part of the helper is appropriate.

(b)   Sharing your feelings. Is it going to be helpful and a good example to your client to tell her how you feel about some aspect of her interview behaviour? Will it destroy rapport? Trust? Adjustment?

There is no doubt that the sharing of feelings can be a positive experience because you can release tensions and feelings which are interfering with your counselling, as can your client. However, the sharing can have negative effects, for example, you may feel so good, that you think this is actually helping the client. Remember the dictum 'helping can be for better or worse!'. Confrontation feedback to a client, according to Simpson (1976) is ill-advised where the following conditions pertain: (Remember, always be cautious.)

Never initiate confrontation feedback where:
1. Your client is known to be emotionally unstable.
2. Your client has daily stresses such that when talking about them, he/she loses control of his/her feelings.
3. Your client has a history of severe emotional reactions.
4. You have doubts, either of your own emotions, or your motives for confronting, or your competence in confrontation.
5. You lack back-up professional services and a case-work supervisor.
6. You are counselling your children.
7. You are counselling physically ill clients.
8. You are working for a voluntary agency that does not allow lay-helpers to explore the emotional life of its clients.

Procedures when initiating confrontation:
(a)   Ask your client if she wants honest feedback (ie. confrontation) eg. do you want to know what I really think about all this? Don't proceed if her voice says 'Yes', but her body-language says 'No!'
(b)   Give small doses in a cautious manner.
(c)   Describe the behaviour or feelings you are concerned with before confronting her about them.
(d)   Emphasise that you are giving a subjective opinion, which may be shared by no-one else.
(e)   Give your feedback tentatively unless you are sure from your experience, that your client can accept otherwise.
(f)   Always build in the idea that people can change, if you are giving feedback that implies the client should change.
(g)   Your confrontation feedback has to be prompt and timely, not relevant to previous times.
(h)   Ask for reactions to your confrontational comments, invite correction, then give your client time to think and answer.

The essence of the above comments is tentativeness on your part, with the emphasis that these are your perceptions which you really want to check out with the client. The way in which this is handled ought to allow the possibility of increasing the area of free activity of the client by, for example, moving material from Cell 2 of the Johari Window, where 'feedback' gives the client the possibility of re-looking at, and re-evaluating her performance. If, in giving feedback the helper can re-frame the essential questions or problems, then this adds immeasurably to the possibility of clients being able to use the feedback without being too defensive. Berenson and Mitchell (1974) describe five types of confrontation or areas in which the client could be challenged.

1. Didactic confrontation: This type of confrontation deals basically with information or misinformation. An example of this is the situation, quoted earlier, where the person being interviewed indicated that there were only three children in the family, and yet there were photographs of four children around the room.

2. Experiential Confrontation: This occurs when the helper experiences the relationship, perhaps in a different way from the client, and draws attention to this, without suggesting that either individual's experiencing is the more correct. These differences in experiencing may occur through discrepancies which can occur between what is said and what is actually done. Furthermore, distortions within the relationship, its purposes and so on may affect the experiencing within the relationship. For instance: I'm afraid of you and therefore, I see you as aloof, although in reality you are a caring person (Egan, 1976).

3. Strength Confrontation: This means pointing out to the client that they have strengths, talents, access to resources and so on but it appears that they are not using them as fully as possible. This is a puzzle, and you wonder why it appears to be the case.

4. Weakness confrontation: This kind of confrontation dwells on the deficits of the person being confronted. Frequently, and unfortunately, this is the preferred mode of operation by many ostensible helpers. The 'deficit' model is popular with politicians, and policy-makers as well as with those in the helping professions. The deficit model focuses on remedying the effects of the deficit and seeks the co-operation of the client in taking action to make up the deficits. It takes courage to be a client, as we have already explored, but deficit confrontation adds to the anxiety and is likely to make clients angry, defensive and less prepared to continue in the relationship. For people with low esteem, like many of our clients, this confrontational approach can be very damaging.

5. Encouragement to action: This is an attempt by the helper to encourage the client to make an impression on the world; to take some kind of control over life. Laudable though this aim is, our clients may not have the capacity, which we as helpers take for granted, to take control over their lives, without a great deal of support as well as encouragement.

Egan (1976) rightly points out that if confrontation is to be for better rather than for worse, then the manner of confrontation is as important as the type. He suggests that confrontation takes place in the spirit of accurate empathy, tentatively, with care, and gradually, depending upon the strength of the relationship. The challenging of the client ought not to stem from our motives to punish the client, but from a desire to be involved with the client at a much deeper level.

In summary, then, confrontation is a technique, a very powerful one, which actively directs your clients to take another look at themselves. There are dangers with its use and as suggested earlier, beginning counsellors ought not to confront their clients as a general rule.

However, beginning helpers can use a number of very worthwhile skills areas as presented in this chapter. These skills areas, if used in a self-conscious style, can be seen to have an effect on the client's behaviour within the counselling session. The distinction between empathy and additive empathy is particularly important, and we raise it again in concluding this chapter. Its importance lies partly in the fact that because, like confrontation, it is a powerful skill, it can be very damaging if misused or badly timed. There is much debate and equivocation about the nature of empathy and whether or not it can be measured (Hornblow, 1980; Yeoman, 1984), but suffice to say that self-conscious practice of skills, with careful perception checking can lead the helper to genuinely experience, and therefore express accurately, empathic responses.

CHAPTER SEVEN

Maintaining the Relationship

7.1 Overview

The skills areas outlined in the previous chapter have relevance for all phases of the contact between helper and client. It must be emphasised that helping occurs in the relationship, and the helper's task is to ensure that the relationship is for better and not for worse. Helpers in the non-medical professions do not have access to drugs or other aids in their helping - the only tool that they have is the relationship they manage to build up with their clients. Helpers may have all the strategies in the world; know all the theories that exist, but if they cannot build up a working relationship with their clients and maintain it, then their work is severely handicapped if not doomed. Note that the emphasis is on a working relationship. A relationship may be warm and friendly and supportive, but this does not necessarily mean that it is a working or an effective relationship.

Felix Biestek, many years ago, outlined what he considered to be the essential elements within a helping relationship. A defect in any one of them, he believed, signified the absence of a good casework relationship. The purpose of the relationship, according to Biestek, is to help the client achieve a better relationship between himself and his environment (Biestek, 1934). This definition closely fits in with the definitions of helping that we have previously used. Biestek's seven principles of the casework relationship will provide the framework for this chapter, in which also will be discussed: Simpson's (1976) ideas concerning some of the conditions which may hinder understanding in interviews; Maslow's (1968) Hierarchy of Needs, and Lewin's (1935) Conflict Theory.

7.2 Principle 1: Individualisation

Individualisation, according to Biestek, is the recognition and understanding of each client's unique qualities, her strengths and weaknesses; her history and development. Each person is individualised by heredity, environment, innate intellectual capacity, and volitional activity. Biestek believes that only as the client feels recognised as a unique individual and feels understood with her problem will she be able to enter into and benefit from a helping relationship.

The implications of the above principle for helpers are quite clear: It implies first of all, a freedom from bias and prejudice. Helpers have to be aware of what Simpson calls the lasting general characteristics of the client: those aspects of the client which cannot be changed and which are an integral part of 'who she is' - for example, the client's ethnic and cultural background, including differences in values and assumptions about the nature of humankind and the world.

Secondly, this principle of individualisation implies the differential use of principles, methods, knowledge and strategies in assisting the client to a better adjustment. Techniques, strategies and so on which were helpful with client 'A' may be inappropriate for client 'B'. To be sure, many clients exhibit similar difficulties, but the assumption can never be made that these are identical or that solutions that were successful in the past will be successful with this particular client, with her particular problems in her unique world.

Biestek argues that common sense may be a great asset in helping, but that this needs to be supplemented by knowledge and insight derived from the sciences. We would go further than this, and argue that the arts, history, literature, and the reflection on our experiencing of life also provide powerful insights which may assist in our work with our clients.

Thirdly, the helper needs, of course, the ability to listen, to observe and to be empathic in the relationship, as has been previously discussed. In addition though, the uniqueness of this client forces the helper to start where the client is and to move at her pace. These are what Simpson calls temporary general characteristics of the client which may affect or dictate the pace at which the client moves. Health problems, fatigue, emotional problems, and stress all play a part in determining how quickly the client will be able to move within a particular interview. Individualisation means a recognition of these temporary states within the client.

Biestek believes that inner conviction is not enough, for individualisation, however. There ought to be a behavioural expression of these inner convictions and attitudes by the helper. This necessary outer expression can be demonstrated by:

1. Thoughtfulness in details - eg. making appointments for a suitable time.
2. Privacy in interviews (though recognising this may be threatening to some ethnic groups)
3. Care in keeping appointments - Be on time!
4. Preparation for interviews - eg. reading records, etc.

Biestek, a Catholic priest, places on the helper an inescapable demand to 'really possess' the appropriate attitudes. This demand permeates all the principles. He believes that if the helper really holds these attitudes - especially 'freedom from bias and prejudice', then the client will sense it, at least intuitively. Any personal or professional deviation from these required attitudes and beliefs will inevitably be transmitted to the client and tend, thereby, to obstruct the development of the helping process.

Biestek believes that clients tend to respond and to react to the 'real' attitudes of the helper. Carl Rogers argues in a similar vein, that if he can create the 'right' genuine atmosphere, display the right kinds of attitudes, then the client will, in a sense, model these in her own life, and be the better for it. Both Rogers and Biestek, however, tend to ignore the fact that the client's response to helping, is at least in part a function of what they bring into the interview in terms of their own attitudes, beliefs, values and so on. There are powerful forces which operate within the client (for example, the Freudian notions of transference and counter-transference) which strongly suggest that clients' responses are not solely the function of helper attitudes and behaviours. Biestek tends to idealise the client in this regard. There is no doubt, however, that clients can sense when the helper is 'putting on an act' and this lack of genuineness, and caring for the client as a unique individual will be reflected inevitably in a relationship that is likely to deteriorate and be 'for the worse'.

7.3   Principle 2: Purposeful Expression of Feelings

This principle focuses on the very human need to be able to express our feelings. Some commentators point out that it is our feelings that make us human! The expression of feelings is important and is a recognition by Biestek that all problems have an emotional tone. No matter how rational we try to be, no matter how dispassionate we are, there is an inevitable tendency to infuse problems and concerns with feelings, with emotions.

The poem in the last chapter points to the legitimacy of owning our feelings - we invest psychic, emotional energy into all aspects of our lives and sometimes, when we are confronted with difficulties and problems, our feelings become heightened. Frequently of course, our feelings 'dominate' the problem, so much so that it often becomes difficult to see the wood for the trees.

The expression of feelings within the helping relationship has to be for a purpose. It is an intentional activity of the helper, and its effect may include release of tension within the client if this is thought appropriate and of benefit for the client (note, not for the benefit of the helper!); so that the helper may understand more fully the problems of the client. Feelings are facts - no-one but the client can tell the helper how he experiences the problems. Many beginning helpers deny or deprecate the feelings that the client is experiencing or has experienced.

Expression of feelings can be a cathartic experience for the client. Having a helper pay attention - listening - to expressions of feelings, hopes and aspirations can not only deepen the relationship but in itself provides psychological support to the client.

Factors which may limit the client's expression of feeling include the agency's role and the stage the client is at in the relationship with the helper. The helper's role is to provide the climate in which expression of feeling by the client may take place - permissiveness, comfort and safety.

Biestek is arguing that human beings have a need to express their feelings. Within a helping interview, a purposeful activity of the helper may be to enable, where appropriate, the client to express her feelings. It may be appropriate for this not to happen - the decision has to be that of the helper; (note, again, the helper, not the client!)

Abraham Maslow (1968) has suggested that needs direct or motivate much of human behaviour. He believes that human needs form a hierarchy, and that the ordering of needs in the pyramid reflect:

1.   the relative potency of the needs - individuals will attempt to satisfy a lower need, like the need for safety before satisfying a need above it, such as self-esteem;

2.   the order in which the needs develop in our lifetime - we are born with only physiological needs and then develop the need to be safe and secure, followed by the needs to be loved, gain self-esteem, and finally push for self-actualisation, which is conceived to be the need to fulfill oneself. It is a need to develop and utilise one's talents, abilities and potential fully 'to become whatever one is capable of becoming';

3. the order in which the needs emerged in the evolution of human beings;

4. the degree to which the need must be satisfied in order to survive.

The needs higher in the hierarchy tend to emerge only as the lower ones become satisfied. The diagram below outlines the Maslow hierarchy. There are two additional needs which seem to be required at all levels within the pyramid. One is the need for information. Frequently, the client will express anger and frustration, the root of which is either a failure to obtain or access the appropriate information or an ignorance that information is available. Secondly, there is a need to obtain mastery and control over the environment. A client becomes a client, as we saw earlier through the actions of others, a continuation of the process which strips away power and control from individuals who have relatively little real control over what happens to them in their day to day living.

Figure 7.1: Maslow's Hierarchy of Needs

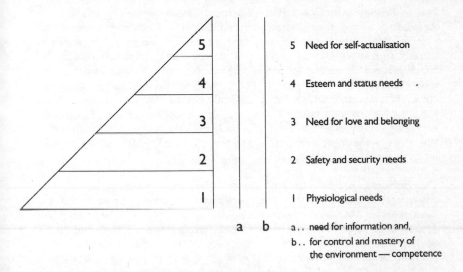

In line with Maslow's ideas, it is unlikely that a client will have his self-esteem needs met (by being treated as a unique individual, by being deemed worthy and prized by the helper) if they are feeling insecure within the relationship. Similarly, unless the basic needs for food, warmth and so on are met, there is little point in attempting to assist the self-actualisation of the client, unless they are becoming a hermit, monk or other religious, whose duty it is to give up all worldly goods, pleasures and so on in the pursuit of their Karma.

It is important to recognise that the needs which people have motivate them to act in order to relieve the tension that the need creates. All people feel threatened when they are unable to meet their needs. Sometimes these needs are not obvious, and frequently, a client's behaviour masks the very needs she is trying to satisfy. Therefore, it is useful to ask yourself, when listening to a client tell her story, a number of questions. For example, one - What needs is she trying to satisfy? Two - What needs are being satisfied at the moment which continue to maintain inappropriate behaviours, attitudes and so on, that are the symptoms of her clienthood? Three - What alternative ways can her needs be met?

The Maslow hierarchy can be a useful way of further understanding your client, and visualising the kinds of priorities people are likely to make in the satisfaction and expression of their needs.

7.4   Principle 3: Controlled Emotional Involvement

As we saw in an earlier chapter, communication is a two way process. Just as the client cannot not behave, neither can the helper. The helper is usually in the position of responding to the client, and this responding takes place at a number of levels (eg. verbal, non-verbal, feelings and emotions). Some clients come to see us with an overwhelming 'emotional tone' surrounding them, and it is difficult not to respond to this in some way, and more difficult to respond to it appropriately. Controlled emotional involvement is Biestek's notion of the helper's sensitivity to the client's feelings; a tentative understanding of their meaning so that he can respond appropriately.

This principle is a corollary of the previous one, and is concerned with the emotional involvement-of the helper with clients, their problems and their worlds. This kind of control really only comes with practice, and experience. It sometimes appears that helpers are callous and 'non-feeling', and whilst this may be a safety device used by the helper to prevent being overwhelmed, a much more pragmatic reason is available. Consider, if the client is overcome by strong emotions, and the helper is caught in this contagion, who then is in a position to be able to stand outside what is happening with any degree of objectivity? Helpers can be caught with their clients in a 'folie-à-deux'. The days have long gone when helpers were cold, overly objective, out-of-vision, non-persons in the encounter with their clients or patients. The focus today is on the helper being a more authentic person in interviews with clients, suggesting a degree of involvement with the client and his pain. The distinction has been made, though, between being involved with the client and being embroiled with the client. The latter indicating a loss of control by the helper where the focus becomes meeting the needs of the helper, rather than those of the client.

Over-involvement with the client or being 'embroiled' with the client can take a number of forms. Obviously, a helper may become sexually involved with a client, and take advantage of the client's vulnerability. Needless to say, this is a complete 'no - no' for helpers.

Secondly, the helper can 'take-over' the problem as their own, denying the client the opportunity to work through this herself. This is inappropriate, for underlying the principle of controlled emotional involvement, is the tacit assumption that the client must own her own problems; that they cannot and should not be taken over by the helper.

There is the apocryphal story of the psychiatrist who became so involved with his client and the fantasy world created by the client, that he looked forward to interviews with this particular client. They, together, could enter the client's universe of make believe. The psychiatrist became so involved with the client that the client's psychosis became his. Relief was at hand, however, when the client announced one day, that he was not coming back to see the psychiatrist, because the psychiatrist was 'mad', and that rather than talk about his problems, all the psychiatrist wanted to do was to become involved in this strange universe. The psychiatrist had to get professional help to escape the psychosis!

Thirdly, the helper can become embroiled with the client through the process of identification, where there is an ostensible similarity of experiencing. For example, a helper who has been through a painful separation and divorce can imagine, falsely, that all divorces and separations are painful. Thus failing to see that this present client's problems and difficulties are not the same. In this situation the helper runs the risk of moving to prescribe ways of dealing with the 'alleged crisis' as he had dealt with it, rather than how the client, being a different person and having a different perspective on the problem could cope with it. This process of identification effectively destroys the possibility of the helper being in control of his own emotional involvement with the client. Bear in mind the comments in the previous chapter relating to the process model of empathy. Identification with the client appears to be a necessary, but not sufficient component of the empathic process. The danger being alluded to here, occurs when there is the failure of the helper to reflect on the nature of the identification

107

with the client. Thus succumbing, and becoming embroiled with the client.

The helper may find for the first time that he has an articulate, educated client. It is a pleasure to work with such a client, so much so that the contact may be unduly prolonged, because both client and helper enjoy their encounter. This kind of embroilment is just as dangerous as the more common embroilments mentioned above. Embroilment (if there is such a word) may reflect the kinds of problems that the helper has not yet worked through for himself!

7.5 Principle 4: Acceptance

This is a principle of action where the helper perceives and deals with the client as she really is (strengths, weaknesses, etc.) maintaining all the while a sense of the client's innate dignity and worth. Although the notion of acceptance has long been one of the most commonly used terms in the helping professions, it has also been one of its most vague. Biestek's carefully developed definition stresses that the object of acceptance is not 'the good' but 'the real'. Acceptance does not mean sanctioning deviant or anti-social attitudes or behaviour. It does mean, though, an unwavering commitment to the innate dignity and worth of people, and to their basic needs and rights. The hierarchy of needs set out by Maslow, gives us a starting place in this sense - our acceptance of clients means we acknowledge the importance of satisfying those needs and believe in the client's rights to do so.

Acceptance, in relation to the Maslovian hierarchy, also recognises that clients will attempt to fulfill lower order needs before higher order ones, and that this is 'OK'. There is little point in trying, for example, to heighten a client's self-esteem if the basic physiological needs for warmth, food, etc., are not met, as mentioned earlier.

This principle also recognises the client's ambivalence about herself, about the coming for help, and about the helper. In general, one assumption that can be made about the client is the likely presence of ambivalence, and helpers must be aware of this and attempt to work with it if the need arises. The ambivalence within the client may on the one hand be a desire to change, because the present state is painful, but on the other hand, may be a recognition that any change will take effort, and why risk the unknown?

Similarly, ambivalence within the helper may occur because of the need to accept where the client is, while, at the same time, recognising the potential within the client, and the need to enable the client to move to where she believes she ought to be!

There are a number of obstacles to acceptance, for example:

1. insufficient knowledge of human behaviour;
2. non-acceptance of something within yourself;
3. imparting (and imputing) own feelings to client;
4. biases and prejudices;
5. unwarranted reassurances;
6. confusion between acceptance and approval;
7. over-identification;
8. loss of respect for the client.

7.6   Principle 5: Non Judgemental Attitude

This principle argues that the quality of the helping relationship is based on the conviction that the helping process excludes the assigning of guilt or innocence, but may include value judgements on attitudes, standards or actions of the client. Many clients come into a relationship in fear of being judged, either in terms of effectiveness in some role (eg. mother), or qualitatively as a person (eg. as unworthy). Passing judgement is not a function of the helping relationship, either of praise or condemnation. But because the helper is presenting reality, or an aspect of reality to the client, the helper has some responsibility to the wider social order. This principle ties in with the previous principle, where in a very real sense you can accept the client as a person, but not his behaviour. Similarly, here, you have a responsibility to see that your own personal integrity as a helper is maintained. Your own particular standards and values must not suffer because of your contact with the client. If you find this difficult then you may have to withdraw from the relationship. Conversely, you may have to withdraw if you find that your values and standards are intruding in some way into the relationship.

More recent workers continue to stress the importance of this principle. Egan (1975) calls it 'suspending critical judgement', listing it as one of the ten major necessary attitudes within the rubric of the principle of 'respect'. Carl Rogers (1951, 1967) argues that the non-judgemental attitude is, in fact, a kind of respect, because it conveys caring which is uncontaminated by evaluations of the client's thoughts, feelings or behaviours.

There are two aspects to the helper's respect for the client encompassed within the term 'non-judgement'. One is the moral notion of placing high value on respect for others without which, we believe, it would seem difficult for anyone to be committed to helping. The other aspect is the recognition that when we convey to another our respect for them, we encourage them to have respect for themselves - self-respect. This, indirectly can facilitate behaviours and attitudes and emotions (including trust in own judgements; risk-taking; self-disclosure and so on) which we have described as being necessary to, and concomitant with, client growth.

Many helpers, however, believe that being non-judgemental means the same as making no judgements. Indeed, many helpers have a laissez-faire attitude to their clients. What is not realised, is that having a laissez-faire attitude is a decision that has been made, and which required the helper to make some judgement. Our concern with self-conscious helping is to encourage the worker to make professional judgements about his client: her needs, strengths, weaknesses, and so on. The helper is called upon to make judgements about the nature of his intervention in the life of the client, which questions to ask, whether to make home visits and so on. So please do not confuse having a non-judgemental attitude to clients with being in the game of not making decisions and judgements!

Embryonic helpers, then, need to be aware that it could be a mistake to believe that having a non-judgemental attitude precludes the making of professional judgements about the client, and thus, may become caught in an inertia which prevents effective action. For example, a person having a low IQ is as a result entitled to the privileges of a special education. It is important, therefore, that this judgement be made, and the options discussed with the parents. To call such a person a 'thick-head' is being judgemental.

We continue to wonder how, for example, government departments, agencies and organisations which refuse to collect data based on ethnic criteria because of its racist overtones, can effectively give differential help to individuals and groups in society while they have no criteria by which to identify those in need. It is like suggesting that data on ages will not be collected from individuals and, therefore, old age pensions can be scrapped!

7.7   Principle 6: Client Self-Determination

This is based on the philosophy that the client (and any person) has an innate ability for self-determination, and that the client has the right to freely make her own decisions. The helper's role is to facilitate the client's seeing her problems more clearly and in perspective. This perspective may include an identification of alternative courses of actions that are available to the client. The helper should also be aware of, and be able to acquaint the client with, community resources which she may be able to utilise and marshal for her benefit. Client self-determination also presupposes that the helper is prepared as far as is possible to stimulate possibly dormant resources within the client and generally create the kind of relationship that will enable the client to grow and work out her own problems. As mentioned earlier, the client is the owner of her problems not the helper, and ultimately it is the client who has to work them out, and to be enabled to live with the decisions made.

There are, of course, limits to the self-determination of the client. The client may not have the requisite resources within herself - her capacity for action may be too limited. Furthermore, there are always civil, moral, legal and social restraints on any action conceived by the client. The nature of the agency for which the helper works may also provide restraints on the client's self-determination.

7.8 Principle 7: Confidentiality

Confidentiality is the preservation of secret information concerning the client which is disclosed in the helping relationship. This has to be subject to both moral and ethical rights and obligations. In Australia, New Zealand and many other Western countries, information disclosed in a helping relationship is not deemed to be privileged communication in the same way as that information disclosed to medical practitioners or to the clergy.

However, confidentiality is considered to be a necessary part of the pursuit of enabling the client to engage in self-exploration. Fear of betrayal may be overcome largely by assurances and demonstrations of confidentiality as a 'professional' ethic. As a professional helper, you may therefore, have on occasions to give very serious consideration to the 'privilege' of having been given private knowledge by the client, and to the wisdom of recording that information, and in what form. Freedom of information legislation suggests that anything that is written down, may in fact be required to be produced in the courts of the land upon request by judicial officials.

There are traps for 'young players' in relation to the notion of confidentiality. Do not be hooked into agreeing to total confidentiality in return for the client telling you something that is 'private' or 'if I tell you this, you won't tell anybody else, will you?'. In most agencies, you cannot guarantee total confidentiality. If you work for any agency, typists, supervisors and maybe even clerks will have access to your client's file, and anything put on file is knowledge within the agency. Clients should be aware of this. Confidentiality cannot be guaranteed, particularly if there is a concern that you have with your client which ought to be shared with other professionals. Obviously, a school-girl cannot be allowed to confide in you to the possible detriment of her parents or guardians. In other words, there are hooks in this notion of confidentiality which need to be borne in mind.

7.9 Lewin's Conflict Theory
Helpers should be aware that clients usually bring with them into the relationship, some degree of ambivalence or conflict. This is almost inevitable. Lewin's Conflict Theory is useful to helpers in that it presents in a very simple form the essential elements within three major types of conflict situations.

7.10 Approach-Approach Conflict
As the name implies, approach-approach conflict occurs when a person has to choose between two positive goals or objectives - goals that are equally attractive at the same time. The girl may have invitations to go out with two boys - Fred and Gary - with whom does she go? The proverbial donkey is supposed to have starved to death because he stood halfway between two piles of hay, and could not decide which he should eat first. Human beings, however, are generally not like donkeys, and our wise girl would probably choose to go out with Fred on Friday night, and with Gary on Saturday night.

Approach-Approach Conflicts usually do not generate much anxiety, as they are relatively easy to resolve. In the diagram below, the individual "P" is confronted by two goals which have only positive characteristics. The distance between the two represents the degree of attraction; in this case, the distances are equal. The choice has to be made! What tends to happen is that the individual has his cake and eats it too! The "+" signs indicate that the goals or objectives are attractive to the individual.

Figure 7.2: **Lewin's Conflict Theory:** Approach — Approach Conflict

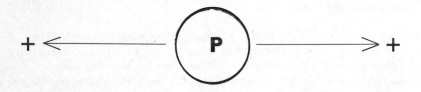

7.11 Avoidance-Avoidance Conflict
This kind of conflict occurs when a person is 'caught between the devil and the deep blue sea'. The choice is between two goals which have negative valences or characteristics, and the individual feels that a choice has to be made. Some examples are: a child must do his homework or get a spanking - neither option is at all attractive; enduring toothache

or going to the dentist; working in a job that is not satisfying or giving it up and risking being unemployed.

Figure 7.3: Lewin's Conflict Theory: Avoidance — Avoidance Conflict

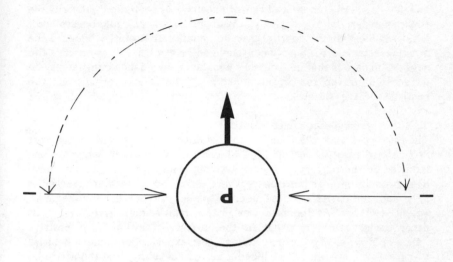

Behaviour in avoidance-avoidance conflict situations is characterised by vacillation and by a tendency to opt out of the situation. The theory postulates that when a person moves towards a goal with negative valence he finds it increasingly repelling. This tends to mean that he will shift back and move towards the other goal which, at a distance, appears to be quite attractive. Again though, as he moves closer to the goal, the negative characteristics become increasingly repellent. The person then wonders if the original goal "A" isn't more attractive, and then moves towards it. But, again as he moves towards "A", it becomes increasingly repellent, and with distance "B" becomes more attractive. Therefore, a person in this kind of conflict will tend to be anxious and will tend to vacillate between the two negative goals. As a result, so much energy gets devoted to this, that the person has, at times, little left for living. A natural consequence may be for the person to opt out of making a decision at all. For example, the child caught between doing homework and being spanked, may decide to run away, or opt out of the situation in some other way.

Helpers can be of assistance to clients in this situation, either by encouraging them and supporting them in making a painful decision, or by enabling the client to discover creative alternatives which effectively by-pass the difficult decision-making. So much of the avoidance-avoidance conflict stems from often illusory arbitrary goals or decisions. Sometimes, being caught in this kind of conflict stems from stereotypic thinking, whereupon a re-definition of the problem may allow the conflict to disappear or to be more easily resolved. If the schoolboy can be enabled to see the homework in a more positive or realistic light, or if the feelings underlying the desire to avoid the homework could be explored, it is possible that the conflict may be handled differently, because the meaning attached to it has been changed or modified in some way. The suggestion here is that unnecessary avoidance-avoidance conflict may be a function of the restricted thinking of the client rather than the realities of the situation.

7.12   Approach-Avoidance Conflict

The third type of conflict, approach-avoidance conflict is often the most difficult to resolve. In this kind of conflict a person is attracted and repelled by the same goal object. A young bride, for example, may have been brought up in an atmosphere where sexual activities were treated as ugly and sinful. As a consequence, sexual matters have a negative valence for her. At the same time, her normal sexual drive, as well as other social values involved in the marital situation have positive valence. Now, as she enters marriage, she experiences anxiety because she is caught between acknowledging her own sexuality and the attitudes learned early in life.

Figure 7.4: Lewin's Conflict Theory: Approach — Avoidance Conflict

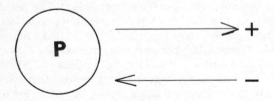

An extension of the approach-avoidance conflict is Double Approach - Double Avoidance Conflict. The following is typical of the internal dialogue an individual may have about the merits or otherwise of changing jobs:

Shall I take a new job in another city? On the one hand, it means promotion, which means eventually more pay and a higher standard of living; plus possibly further promotion, and even more enhanced status. It also means the need to make new friends. But this means giving up old friends, and whilst the children would get into possibly better schools, they will leave schools where they are doing OK, plus they will be losing their old friends. Then there is the packing and the shifting! Will my partner be able to find work.

Figure 7.5: Lewin's Conflict Theory: Double Approach — Double Avoidance Conflict

There are a great many pros and cons to be weighed up in a situation like this. A very difficult decision has to be made one way or the other. Double Approach- Double Avoidance conflict situations are very common in everyday life.

There is always an opportunity-cost, and losses of one kind or another are involved. The task here, perhaps, is to minimise the costs involved whichever decision is made. The helper should recognise that where loss occurs, or where separation is involved, then grieving may take place. The grieving could well take place before the decision has been made. Helpers ought to be aware that anticipatory grieving may be inhibiting decision-making and the resolution of the conflict.

7.13   Force-Field Analysis
One way in which these approach-avoidance conflicts can be tackled, is by the use of what Egan calls 'Force-Field Analysis' (Egan, 1975). The

helper assists the client in clarifying the nature of the problems, and identifying what are basically the pros and cons. Then the helper assists the client to set priorities for the solution of the problems, the order in which the problems are to be tackled. The client is then asked to decide what are the outcomes which he would prefer, among a range of outcomes. This is followed by the setting up of some workable goals for the client. Obviously there needs to be congruence between the attainable goals and the outcomes sought by the client. Clients frequently need the outcomes they seek translated into concrete, immediately attainable objectives. (Note, the broad similarities with the Mandala mapping technique).

Next, the client is encouraged to list all the possible means of attaining that goal, and again, the pros and cons for each course of action are explored. The helper then attempts to work with the client to make the pros more attractive and the cons less repelling.

Egan (1975) puts it like this:

> Force-field analysis is a sophisticated term for a process that is, conceptually at least, relatively simple. Basically it means this: John has a problem. The solution to that problem is his goal. Once he sees what his goal is, he sees what forces keep him from his goal (restraining forces) and what forces help move him toward his goal (facilitating forces). He then determines what courses of action will help him decrease the strength of the restraining forces and increase the strength of the facilitating forces. He chooses those means that are most practical and that are in tune with his personal values. Finally, he implements these means and evaluates his progress. If the means he chooses are inadequate, he chooses other means by the same process until he reaches his goal or sees that it is impossible.

Egan sees the field as a kind of battleground on which the client struggles to live more effectively. He believes that the method is systematic, and therefore, involves well-defined, concrete steps. These steps are summarised as follows. The helper should help the client to:

> 1. Identify and clarify the problems in the client's life.
> 2. Establish priorities; that is, determine which problem is to receive immediate attention. Don't help the client defeat himself by having him work on too many problems at the same time.
> 3. Establish concrete, workable goals, to which the client is committed.

4. Take as complete a census as possible of the means available for achieving each concrete goal. List concrete ways of instituting and strengthening facilitating forces and of weakening or eliminating restraining forces.

5. Choose the means that are in keeping with the client's value system and that will most effectively help him achieve established goals.

6. Establish criteria by which the effectiveness of action programmes can be evaluated.

7. Implement: use chosen means to achieve established goals.

8. Review and evaluate the client's progress. (Egan, 1975).

As mentioned earlier, there are broad similarities between the above systematic way of helping clients and the Mandala mapping procedure outlined earlier. In addition, there are similarities between the above, our flow-diagram of the helping procedure, and also Glasser's Reality Therapy. The point being made here, is that practitioners from a variety of perspectives tend to have common views of the helping process.

Biestek's principles will enable you to keep a check on your activity as the helper in the relationship, and should assist in the maintenance of a good relationship between yourself and the client. Due recognition of the insights of Maslow and Lewin should also enable you to be more sensitive to the needs of clients and to recognise some of the conflicts they face. The force-field analysis model of Egan should assist in providing you with some way of assisting the client make some progress in the solution of her problems.

Other strategies utilised in this phase of the relationship include the idea of behavioural contracts; role playing; modelling; empty-seat technique and so on.

7.14   Contracting

A contract is an agreement between the helper and the client (or between partners; or between the school and a pupil) in which one party to the contract agrees to do certain things; change certain behaviours. The consideration for such changes may be for the other party to the contract to also make some changes, or forgo some action that could be taken. For example, Jonny wants to stay in his present class; this could be made dependent on his more regularly doing homework.

Mr Smith complains that his wife nags him all the time; his wife states that he is never home, and when he is, he never listens to her. A contract in writing could be drawn up between them that might list the behaviours she expects from him: ie. listen to me when I talk about the kids; stay home

117

three nights of the week. He would also list the behaviours he expects of her. Once these are mutually agreed to, the contract would come into force, and would be monitored by the helper. The ownership of the problem lies with the client or clients, and the client has to work at it to arrive at some solution with the assistance and support of the helper.

7.15   Role Playing

Role playing may take several forms, but usually involves the client playing one or both of the actors (in turn) in a problem situation. This may be used to try-out (rehearse) behaviours or new strategies of coping with the problem. Or, by using role-reversal, the client becomes the other person in the problem arena, with the helper taking the role of the client. The client (as the other) is then exposed to her own behaviour as portrayed by the helper. It may give the client some insight into how the other person in the situation may experience the problem. In either case, the helper is enabling the client to obtain a wider perspective of the problem, and thus, hopefully increase the possibilities for effective action.

7.16   Empty-Seat Technique

This is a technique whereby the client expresses herself to a person who is not present, but who is thought to be occupying the empty seat. It may help to shed some of the 'unfinished business' that the client has with the person concerned. For example, if a parent is dead, and the client has had some difficulty expressing her feelings to the deceased parent, the empty chair provides the opportunity for her to say the things directly that, perhaps, could have been, but never were said whilst that parent was alive. This is self-disclosure.

The empty-seat technique has to be used with care. It can provoke very strong emotional outbursts from the client, particularly where there is 'unfinished business'. Like role-playing it can be used to rehearse scenes with the boss, the partner and so on and provides an opportunity to hear what it sounds like! This is analogous to the moving of material from the 'Blind Cell' within the Johari window in the area of 'Free Activity'. In that sense, it becomes public knowledge and thus, is far more within the control of the client. Furthermore, the rehearsal provides the client with the possibility of additional feedback from the helper.

7.17   Concluding Comments

This chapter has provided you, the helper, with an introduction to a wide variety of theories, models and possibilities for assisting the client. You have to be creative in the way you use the knowledge of the world, of the social sciences, literature and arts. But underlying all this, has to be a fundamental caring, encapsulated to some extent in the ideas of Biestek, and Yeoman (1984).

But having said that, caring by itself is not sufficient. This chapter we believe, gives some ideas for purposeful, informed self-conscious practice and action.

CHAPTER EIGHT

Terminating the Relationship

8.1 Overview
As the helper moves through the helping process with the client, it becomes inevitable that the relationship must come to an end. In this chapter, we will outline the three kinds of termination suggested by Okun (1976) and add a fourth, the termination of contact through the referral of the client to another organisation, helper or agency. The helper has to have the ability to 'let go' and the client needs to feel confident enough to be able to detach himself from the helper. As the separation and the ending of the relationship may involve some sadness and grieving, helpers need to be aware of the processes of grieving. These processes will be briefly outlined in this chapter, particularly the ideas of Lindemann (1944) and Kubler-Ross (1969). The chapter will conclude with a brief discussion of the need for and the nature of evaluation. You will recall that in the flow diagram of the helping process, not only ought there to be an evaluation of the client's performance, but the helper's activity in the relationship also should be evaluated.

8.2 Mutually Ending the Contact
An effective helper will ensure that the client is helped as quickly and as effectively as possible. Stewart et al.(1978) argue that the helper must be concerned about efficiency in helping as well as relationship development and outcomes. They suggest that there is not enough time to continue to meet and talk on a regular basis with a client once the agreed goals have been reached. Contact with the client should, therefore, not be prolonged unduly. In most cases, the completion of agreed tasks is a signal to both parties in the helping relationship that contact between them should be, and is indeed, ended.

The helper should recognise that any kind of parting, particularly after a therapeutic encounter, may provoke feelings of loss and grief. These sad feelings usually afflict both the helper and the client. Okun suggests that where these feelings are freely expressed and the meanings explored then the termination process may in fact be a period of growth for both helper and client.

Where both parties agree that contact between the parties should cease because mutually agreed goals and objectives have been met, then the satisfaction in the achievement of common goals should be freely acknowledged by both helper and client. Where contact between the helper and the client mutually ends and commonly agreed goals and objectives have not been met, this should be clearly articulated, and possibly explored. This mutual termination can occur when it was initially agreed that contact should be only for a specified number of interview hours.

The failure to reach stated objectives may be a function of a number of factors, and time ought to be taken out to explore the reasons for not reaching agreed objectives. This process of exploration again provides the opportunity for growth for both parties, provided that the evaluation is carried out in a constructive manner. The atmosphere should not be acrimonious, and blaming ought not to be countenanced during this process. Of course, it may well be that the objectives as originally outlined were unrealistic, and this ought to be acknowledged. The evaluation process, regardless of the nature of the termination ought to be conducted as honestly as possible.

8.3   Termination by the Client

Social exchange theory considers that people will continue a relationship if needs are being met in some degree within the relationship, or that the perceived costs of leaving the relationship are greater than the costs of remaining in the relationship. Witness to this is, of course, the large number of people who persist in marriages which, apparently on the surface, should have been finished a long time ago. There is a tendency, then, for relationships to persist even when the rewards for remaining within the relationship appear to be minimal. In professional, ostensibly therapeutic relationships envisaged under the rubric of 'helping', this may also be the case.

Helpers need, on the one hand, to be aware of the likely persistence of a relationship beyond the optimum number of interviews, where marginal gains are minimal. On the other hand, helpers need to explore the reasons where a client moves against the inertia of not terminating contact, particularly if the relationship has been a long-standing one.

Many clients terminate helping relationships because they feel that they are getting little out of the relationship - it is not meeting their needs in some way. The client may, for example, feel threatened in some way and opt out of the situation, as suggested by Lewin's Conflict Theory. In such cases, the helper may feel useless and inadequate.

Where the client suggests premature termination, Okun believes that it is crucial for the helper to really listen closely to the client, to determine whose problem this is; it might be the client's, if he is refusing to work further and chooses avoidance rather than approach procedures. On the other hand, it may be the helper's problem, perhaps in demanding too much from the client; or perhaps, in failing to build a solid relationship which is effective and flexible.

Frequently clients will hint that they are considering a move away from the helping relationship, by introducing irrelevant topics for discussion; commenting on aspects of living, etc. which have little to do with the reason for the relationship. One self-help group, in which one of the writers was involved, was seen to come to an end when members of the group moved away from a discussion of group dynamics and the group experience, as experienced by members of the group, and started discussing salary and the conditions of employment of counsellors and social workers. This shift in the nature of the 'group talk' was evidence that the raison d'etre of the group had disappeared.   The group did not meet again!

There is a wealth of research that many clients do not return after the first interview. This failure to make further contact may mean that the helper and the agency ought to look at their intake procedures. If one helper in an agency has a higher rate of non-returns than other helpers, then this ought to be explored with the helper concerned. Ellis (1973) as part of his Rational Emotive Therapy, gives his clients 'homework' and this seems to act as an incentive to return. Clients ought to be encouraged to return, especially if their needs for help are great. Of course, the client tends to use the first interview to make decisions about whether or not they will return; whether they believe that the helper will be able to help them. This is, of course, indicative of the crucial importance of the first interview.

8.4   Termination by the Helper

Termination initiated by the helper may occur as a result of factors outside of the relationship, eg. limits placed on counselling by term dates, or because of personal changes within an agency. Termination may be also initiated by the helper if he believes that he is unlikely to build a good relationship with the client. While it is not expected that helpers will like everybody they meet, it can happen that a strong disliking may prevent the development of a good working relationship with the client.

In a situation like this, helpers should express dissatisfaction about their ability to build a relationship, and wonder, out aloud, how it can be improved. The client may be forthcoming, and this could be a very worthwhile growth experience for the helper. Where the helper believes that the contact should be ended, the feelings of the client have to be recognised and worked with. The client may feel that the contact is being terminated because he is not liked, so work in this case must be orientated towards alleviating any undue feelings of rejection. Sometimes clients will express anxiety about the possibility that their problems are too severe, that nothing can be done for them and hence, there is unlikely to be any solution to their problems. As well, the helper has to recognise that their clients may feel anger concerning the breakup of the relationship, and must be prepared to explore these feelings with the client.

8.5   Preparation for Ending the Helping Relationship
The helper has a duty to assist the client with the task of ending the helping relationship, and some helpers give advance notice of termination. Others begin to space out contacts with their clients, so that whilst meeting with them on a regular basis, the frequency of contact may diminish from once a week, to once a fortnight; monthly and so on.

Helpers should be aware that many clients' dependency needs are strong, and that they will go to great lengths to prolong relationships. If this occurs, then the helper must look very carefully at the nature of the relationship built up with the client over time; the goals set within the relationship; and the nature of the agreed limits on the relationship. The setting of limits is important in helping, particularly in terms of the time available for your client. Clients can become most unrealistic, and setting limits helps to face them with the real world. Always, however, leave the door open for the client to re-contact you if necessary.

8.6   Referral
Referral is a special case of termination of contact, and occurs when it is decided that another person or agency should be brought into the helping process. It may be that the initial contact with yourself or your agency was inappropriate and that the client may be better served by being referred on. If this is decided, then an early referral is called for. This is because many referrals take time, and it may be appropriate for the helper to keep contact with the client in a supportive role to bridge the time. Sometimes clients are reluctant to accept a referral, and this acceptance may then become a goal of your helping relationship with the client.

When making a referral to another agency, it is important that you send the appropriate details and records to the new agency or helper. What may be appropriate to send on, in a particular case, has to be the professional, caring judgement of the helper. In most cases, the client should be a full party to the referral decision, and should have a role in deciding what material should be passed on to the new agency, helper or organisation. It is important to consider the possibility of a follow-up after the referral has been made. This should be with the agency to whom the referral has been made, and not to the individual client. If the agency report that no contact was made, then you may decide to follow-up with the client directly. In all cases of follow-up checks, great tact and sensitivity should be shown.

8.7   Use of Community Resources

Effective referral requires among other things, an intimate knowledge of the resources available in your community. It is imperative that helpers know not only the helping organisations within their community, but also key individuals within agencies and the community. This will enable helpers to make differential referrals depending upon the needs of their client. 'Differential' referral means that helpers must know to which agency, organisation, and/or individual they can make a referral in a particular case, and those which are contra-indicated. Helpers must be aware of what they know and what they don't know!

The following questions are posed as an attempt to motivate the helper to be conscious that a network of contacts, a personal 'grapevine' is very important in the practice of self-conscious helping. This is because, as you become aware of your own limitations in your helping practice, you are more likely to refer the client on, if it is in the best interests of your client. To be sure, there are many times we continue to work with clients who ought to be referred on, but this is impossible where the resources are not available. So....

1.   How well do you know your local community?
2.   Who are its leaders?   This is particularly relevant where the community has a broad ethnic diversity. Are there factions within any one ethnic group?
3.   Who can be trusted in your community; within any ethnic group?
4.   How effective are the various agencies and organisations in meeting the needs of its clients?
5.   What kinds of problems do these agencies and organisations have which may affect their effectiveness?
6.   Are there individuals within an organisation that you respect for their professionalism, who may be helpful, despite

the agency or organisation they work for?
7. Is the turnover of staff within organisations you usually work with a concern?
8. Who can you go to for professional advice and supervision, perhaps, in an informal way?

In most large cities throughout the world, there exist directories of local organisations and agencies, and any such directory could provide a good starting place for gaining the knowledge required to make effective and efficient referrals. Helpers should endeavour to develop a personal and a professional network of contacts with other helpers and individuals in the community, whom they trust as fellow professionals, for the purposes of effective and appropriate referrals and broader based helping activities and professional development.

8.8 Grief Work

Eric Lindemann (1944) stressed the importance of 'grief work' which allows the bereaved to rework the past and cut ties with the deceased sufficiently to be able to build new relations and a new life. When people do not engage in 'grief work' following any profound loss, serious emotional, mental, and social problems can occur. The profound loss need not necessarily occur through physical death, but may occur as a result of separation, or any kind of change in life-space, which necessitates substantial re-organisation or re-orientation of personal life. For example, children may need to grieve if a favourite possession is lost or a family pet dies. The separation or loss may be symbolic rather than physical, for example a friend of the writers' mourned for a considerable period of time when he attained fifty years of age. He remarked that he had been on this earth for fifty years and achieved nothing. The depth of his depression was profound.

Normal 'grief work' as defined by Eric Lindemann, consists of four major stages:

1. Acceptance of the pain or loss.
This according to Lindemann, means dealing with the memory one has of the deceased, or loss. Helpers frequently have difficulty in deciding whether or not a topic relating to the deceased ought to be broached. And yet, it seems to us, a matter of fact approach, with sensitivity, of course may be useful to the client in the coming to terms with the loss.
2. Open expression of pain, sorrow, hostility and guilt.
The person must feel free to mourn openly his loss, usually by weeping, and to express any feelings of guilt or hostility. Helpers must be aware, however, that there may be cultural and sub-cultural expressions of grief or, reactions to loss which are markedly different from their own. One

funeral service, which one of the authors attended, comprised hymns of jubilation and happiness that the deceased had gone to heaven. Quite different from the sorts of funeral service normally encountered!

3. Understanding the intense feelings associated with the loss.

Understanding the intense feelings, may include a recognition by the helper, that the bereaved may have fears of insanity, inadequacy, 'lostness', and that these may be the result of the grieving process. When these feelings of sorrow, fear and guilt are worked through in the presence of a caring person, their potency gradually subsides. Ritual expressions of grief or loss in funerals, retirement functions and their like, may greatly aid the grieving process.

4. Eventual resumption of normal activities and social relationships.

Time is a great helper, provided the grief process is being worked through. Gradually the depression begins to lift and there is a resurgence of hope, with the realisation that life has to go on. It is a time for the building of new attachments and new relationships.

The Kubler-Ross (1969) theory of 'dying' follows a similar pattern. In her theory, however, those who are dying pass through five stages. Not everyone goes through all the stages, and there may be some slipping backwards and forwards between stages. In fact, a person can be in more than one of her stages at any given time.

The first stage is one of **denial.** Individuals in this stage resist acknowledging the reality of the impending death, loss or separation, as the case may be. The denial is functional in that it gives time for the client or individual to come to terms with what may be happening to them or to someone they love. Prolonged denial, of course, may well be dysfunctional, and has to be watched. Clients or individuals going through the denial stage, are in effect saying 'NO' this is not happening, or more realistically, 'this cannot be happening!'.

Anger is the next stage. Dying people ask the question, 'Why me?' They may look at the persons around them and feel envy, jealousy,and rage over the health and vigour of others. During this phase, a dying person often makes life difficult for others, criticising friends, family, and medical personnel with little justification. For any client or individual undergoing a 'dying process' or mourning any loss or separation, the helper needs to recognise that the anger may be expressed in many forms, and may be random in terms of the target to which it is directed. The anger, however expressed, may be an indication to the helper that the client has moved, or is moving through the 'denial' stage, and is suggestive of a movement towards an acceptance of the loss.

Bargaining is the middle stage of the process. Dying individuals, and those experiencing loss of any kind, may frequently bargain with God, fate, or the illness itself, hoping to arrange a temporary truce; a moratorium during which time certain tasks can be completed. Furthermore, there is frequently a belief, a hope, that the truce will in itself resolve the problem, that somehow or other, God, or with whomsoever the bargain has been made, will forget, and the problem, the loss, or illness will disappear. In exchange for the time extension, the client will promise to be 'good' or to do something constructive with the time left to them. For instance an individual will plead, saying 'Just let me live long enough to attend my son's marriage', or 'Allow me to get my business in order'.

The 'bargain' generally is successful for only a short period, since the advance of the illness itself, or the inevitability of the change invalidates the 'agreement.' This produces a new stage, that of **depression.** Dying people begin to mourn their own deaths, the loss of all the people and things they have found meaningful, and the plans and dreams never to be fulfilled - they experience what Kubler-Ross terms "preparatory grief".

Helpers must recognise that depression is one of the more common symptoms of loss, or an indication that grieving is taking place. The grieving may, in a middle-aged person, be for the loss, or recognition of the loss of potential: that the hopes that they had for their career have not been realised; that they are not going to be famous, etc. Adolescents may become depressed upon leaving school, and this may hinder their transition into the work force. Children may become depressed if their favourite toy is lost.

The last stage is one of **acceptance.** The dying have by this time mourned their impending loss, and they begin to contemplate the coming of the end with a degree of quiet expectation. In most cases they are tired and quite weak. They no longer struggle against death but make their peace with it.

Acceptance should not be mistaken for a happy stage. It is almost void of feelings. It is as if the pain had gone, the struggle is over, and there comes a time for 'the final rest before the long journey,' as one patient phrased it. Acceptance can be hindered if loved ones or associates are themselves in the 'denial' stage. Helpers need to be aware that the families of the dying mis-guidedly, sometimes, for reasons of guilt, their own sense of loss, rekindle hope in the person who has otherwise moved into the final stage. The sadness of this lies in the fact that it generates an uneasiness in the dying patient which is carried into death, at a time when the work of accepting their own demise had been accomplished. Families need to be helped to recognise, and to do their own 'grief work' more or less in conjunction with the dying.

The psychologist Robert Kastenbaum points out that although Kubler-Ross's theory has merit, it neglects certain aspects of the death process. One of the most important is the nature of the disease itself, which greatly affects pain, mobility, the length of the terminal period, and the like (Kastenbaum, 1975).

The point is that the Kubler-Ross model describes the kinds of stages she observed in patients dying of cancer. This in itself is a great achievement. What we have tried to do is to suggest that the model can be generalised to all situations in which there is a degree of loss or change in life-space. The Kastenbaum critique of the Kubler-Ross model is quite valid and interested readers are referred to his work. Nonetheless, it may be helpful for helpers to use the model, being aware that there are dangers in its use.

There are parallels to the work of Lindeman and Kubler-Ross and in the writings of Bowlby (1960) on separation anxiety, and such parallels lend a degree of legitimacy not to be ignored.

The final activity in any work with a client is an evaluation of the work of the helper in relation to the contact with the client which has just been finalised. This review of the work with the client obviously should include the joint assessment of how well the client has done in relation to mutually agreed goals and objectives. The review should also include some statement of how the processes of separation were handled, and an indication of the growth that emerged from the opportunity offered by the termination of the contact.

8.9   Review and Evaluation of the Work with the Client

This aspect of the work of the helper is probably the most neglected. Yet, we believe that it is probably the most important for the development of self-conscious helping. Within the relationship, there has to be a continuous review and monitoring of the process to ensure that the client's needs are being met. This process is for the benefit of the client. The final evaluation, on the other hand, is for the improvement of the quality of the service offered by the helper.

The mistakes, the bungles, the errors of judgement and actions are the source of the future growth of the helper. This suggests that the helping relationship should be examined honestly. Where you believe you did well, examine these aspects closely also. For here may be the clues that point to genuine helping, that the helper may be able to use across clients in a variety of contexts. For example, the helper may find that certain kinds of feedback appear to enable the client do a great deal of work; it may be that the judicial use of silence was extremely powerful in assisting the client to work through her problems. Helpers should search their behaviour and performance in interviews for those things that are really helpful, as well as for those areas in which mistakes were made. A careful scrutiny of helper performance can only improve the quality of the service to clients and is in line with the thesis of self-conscious helping. The problems encountered and not overcome should be examined and explored carefully. Helpers may find it useful to set out alternatives they could have attempted and which might not have been so problematical.

The evaluation process can be aided by the development of rating scales and other psychometric instruments which may give some relatively objective feedback on helper performance as well as on the progress being made by the client. In attempting to measure change within clients over time, it must be remembered, however, that 'difference scores' (ie. the difference between scores obtained on a measure at the beginning of contact, and those obtained towards the end) are notoriously unstable. Clients, in other words, will have to make large 'difference scores' in order for you to feel confident that the difference in scores obtained is a real difference and not an artifact of chance. We believe that the collection of such data on clients can aid in your professional development. For example, if one of the fundamental beliefs is that helping should enhance self esteem in clients, and you find that over a period of time, with a number of clients your work with them is not resulting in a growth of self esteem, then you need either to change your belief system, or more importantly, examine the nature of your work with clients carefully to discover why it is that growth in self esteem is not occurring.

Barrett-Lennard (1962) developed a relationship inventory which ostensibly measures five of the facilitative conditions of interpersonal relationship deemed necessary for interpersonal growth, including congruence, willingness to be known (self disclosure), level of regard, and empathic understanding. This scale has recently been revised. It appears to be both a reliable and valid instrument for its particular purposes (see Gurman, 1977 for a review of the scale). Some items from this scale are included here to give some understanding of their nature. The instrument is completed by both the helper and the client, and the two sets of perceptions compared. This procedure can faciliate a useful dialogue between helper and client.

Here are some of the items from the Barrett-Lennard scale (male counsellor - client form). He used a six point scale (strongly agree,

agree, mildly agree, mildly disagree, disagree, strongly disagree). The helper and the client, using separate forms, circle the appropriate category in response to the item:

- He respects me
- He tries to see things through my eyes
- He pretends that he likes me or understands me more than he really does
- His interest in me depends partly on what I am talking to him about
- He dissaproves of me
- He understands my words but not the way I feel
- He is interested in knowing what my experiences mean to me
- What he says to me never conflicts with what he thinks or feels
- His feeling to me does not depend on how I am feeling towards him
- He is disturbed whenever I talk about or ask about certain things.

A number of scales have been developed as an outcome of the work of Truax and Carkhuff (1967). Some recent research by Yeoman (1984), however, suggests that while the Truax/Carkhuff Empathy Scale may be extremely reliable (that is, scores obtained on one administration of the test are similar to those obtained by the same people on subsequent administrations), whether or not it is valid, (ie. measures empathy) is a moot point.

The following is an extract from an Empathy Rating Scale along the lines suggested by Truax and Carkhuff. Raters are asked to rate the quality of helper responses to clients' statements (on, in this case a seven level scale). It is, therefore, a rating scale of helper responses, and before the responses are rated, the raters are instructed to take into account the context in which the response was given.

> Therefore, examine closely what was said prior to the worker
> making the 'empathic' statement or response, to determine
> how well tuned in, the worker was to what the client was
> saying'. Rate the worker on the following seven point scale.
> (Yeoman, 1984).

We have included only levels One, Three, Five and Seven and these are sufficient to give you the flavour of the scale.

Level One: The worker is overtly destructive in the interviewing process, and fails to attend (sharp body shifts, major topic jumps, etc) in a way that disrupts the client flow, or attacks the client or discounts information or feelings.

Level Three: At first glance the session appears to be going OK. But, on a closer analysis, the worker is undermining, detracting the client in often a minimal way. The paraphrasing is close, but is missing the point, and what is happening is that things within the worker are distorting what it is the client is saying. The client is not damaged and has been listened to minimally.

Level Five: There is something that is added, comments and responses are not merely interchangeable. This is often in the form of an interpretation, or suggestion that there are other ways of looking at what the client is saying. This something, which is added, facilitates further growth and exploration.

Level Seven: Hoped for by many, attained by few. This level is characterised by the worker really being with the client; being part of the client, but apart from the client. Direct, mutual communication is shown at this stage in its full dimensions.

The following is a very simple scale which was developed by Yeoman (1984). It is completed by both the helper and the client (with of course appropriate changes in words!), who have to circle the number of the response which best represents their view.

How helpful has this session been to you?

1. Extremely harmful
2. Harmed me quite a lot
3. Moderately harmful
4. Slightly more harmful than helpful
5. Indifferent - a waste of time - neither helpful nor harmful
6. Slightly more helpful than harmful
7. Moderately helpful
8. Helped me quite a lot
9. Extremely helpful

We suggest that, if you use the above scale you might like to seek the reasons why the client felt as she did, and also, it would be useful to obtain the helper's reasons as well. The nine point scale could be used with other questions such as: 'How much insight did you gain into your difficulties from this session?' or, 'How helpful was this session to you in determining what you should do next?'

We are suggesting that the helper evaluation can be aided by the use of self-made instruments or those devised and constructed by theoreticians and practitioners. Similarly discussing your work with a supervisor on a regular basis throughout the course of your work with a client can be most beneficial for you and for your client. This benefit can be enhanced if the helper prepares a written overview of the case upon its completion for discussion with the supervisor. Some agencies provide for the video-taping of interviews and for the opportunity to have the interview tapes critiqued by others in the agency. Whilst this can be daunting for the helper concerned, it is essential that they open up their work for professional, caring scrutiny, in the interests both of their professional development as helpers and hence, subsequent benefit to clients, and also for the protection of the agency and the profession.

1. **I react to conflict and antagonism from others with tolerance**
   Never _____Always

2. **I perceive myself as being understanding of others' needs**
   Never _____Always

3. **I respect the values of others**
   Always _____Never

4. **I am able to express my thoughts and feelings**
   Always _____Never

5. **I am able to assert myself with other people**
   Never _____Always

6. **I am aware of my strengths and weaknesses**
   Always _____Never

7. **I am able to understand my feelings and needs**
   Never _____Always

The above are a few items from a Counselling Skills and Values Check List which can be used by the helper in conjuction with his supervisor. Each completes it, separately, by checking the point in the line which best represents his view. Then, the two forms are compared and any major discrepancies between the two sets of perceptions are discussed.

A helper and his supervisor can devise an instrument along the lines suggested above. It is relatively easy to generate items which reflect the agency's values and organisational requirements; for example, an item might be 'I get my work done on time' - Never. . . Always. It is suggested that an instrument with about twenty items would be sufficiently long for most agencies' needs. Items could be grouped into areas of interest - for example, you might want five items to be concerned with values; five items related to administrative requirements and perhaps, ten items related to specific skill development, and so on. The limitations on the design of this kind of instrument are only those of the imagination.

Other kinds of evaluation involve the agency getting in touch with the client some weeks after contact has been terminated, to ascertain how the client is getting on (demonstration of caring) and to obtain some feedback on the performance of the agency and the helper. In this way, clients tend to be more objective and feel less threatened in making comments. It also means that the work of the helper can be judged in terms of its likely future impact on clients, following the cessation of· contact. Typically, if there is to be a renewal of contact, then this is likely to take place within a month. One of the writer's students surveyed the clients of a vocational guidance agency approximately two years after contact had been terminated. Some clients could not even remember being clients of the agency concerned, and the general consensus was that the contact had not been too helpful. In current research being undertaken by one of the writers, the vocational guidance agencies both private and governmental were not rated highly as being very helpful. Indeed, the opposite was the case, they were detrimental to the clients concerned.

Maybe, it is because of these kinds of results that helpers tend to neglect to evaluate their own work. Certainly, questions can be raised about whether or not clients are in a position to evaluate the work of helpers, but surely, many of the items above could be used by most helpers.

There is a caveat, however. It must be recognised that many of the items are value laden (towards the notion of self-conscious helping?) and you may disagree with the items and wonder about their relevance and importance in helping. This would depend on the kinds of values you hold as a helper. But, if you are aware of those values, ie self-conscious, then you are in a position to devise ways and means of evaluating your competence as a helper. In our view, evaluation of helper performance is crucial to enhanced helper competence and effectiveness, and is in line with our notion of the self-conscious helper. We would argue that if you are not prepared to spend time evaluating your work as a helper, then perhaps, you should consider moving out of helping

CHAPTER NINE

Crisis Counselling

9.1　What is a Crisis?

Hansell (1976) defines a crisis as 'any rapid change or type of encounter which is very much outside a person's usual range of experience'. Many of our clients are in this situation - how many times have you heard a person say, for example, 'I didn't know what to do next'. It seems as though the strangeness of the event or incident temporarily throws the client off balance -   so much so, that the old ways of coping, or strategies for overcoming the problem do not seem to work.

Hoff (1978) views the nature of crises somewhat differently. She recognises that stressful events and emergency situations are a part of life, and always have the potential of becoming a crisis. She points out that what may be a crisis for you, may not be a crisis for me, and therefore helpers need to be aware that crisis occurs when our interpretation of these events leads to stress so severe that we can find no relief. A crisis then occurs in the eye of the beholder, and it is not for the helper to argue whether or not the situation in which a client finds himself is a crisis. A crisis for many individuals represents a call to new action which they cannot face with their present resources. While a crisis often has connotations of fear and anxiety, it also has the opportunity for growth. As such, crises are a part of the fabric of life.

Adams et al. (1976) talk about transitions in terms of changes in life-space, or as discontinuities provoking the necessity for change. Typical of these are the life-stage transitions, for example, moving from school to work, marriage, divorce, retirement, the first child, and so on. These life-events, as Holmes and Rahe (1967) call them, have an impact on our life-space and inherently call for change in behaviour, perceptions, attitudes and so on. The severity of the transition or discontinuity may be such, and sufficiently acute to come into the category of crisis.

We believe that an understanding of the crisis process is essential for helpers as they attempt to help clients cope with crisis. Many of our clients seem to live crisis-ridden lives, moving from one catastrophe to another. Some individuals do seem to thrive on the anxiety and the tension and may provoke crisis situations for the excitement. We need to be careful that in our work as helpers we do not provoke clients or crises, to meet our needs, whether this is for the 'excitement' or for the satisfaction of being wanted, or of needing to be the St. George who can slay the 'crisis' dragon!

9.2   The Crisis Process

Caplan (1964) identifies four phases which he believes characterise the crisis process. Phase 1 is some traumatic event, which causes a rise in an individual's anxiety level; and to which the individual responds in his usual way.

This may escalate further (Phase 2), if the individual finds that his ways of coping which have generally been successful in the past, no longer work. The failure of the old ways of coping may result in increased anger and frustration, as well as a lowering of self esteem, and there tends to be an accompanying increase in the level of anxiety.

During Phase 3, the individual begins to search for new strategies or even solutions to diminish the ever-rising anxiety. It may be that during this phase, the problem becomes re-defined; for example, by shifting the blame for the problem or crisis away from the self to another person, or to an external agency (the firm was losing money, so they had to get rid of me. . . the truth, in this case, has to do with the person's incompetence which he would rather not have to face). It may be, for example, that the individual will opt out of the field, as is common in avoidance-avoidance conflict. If support within the family and community is lacking or, if the client's attempts to seek new solutions to the problem are not found, Caplan believes that Phase 4 of the crisis process is reached.

Phase 4 is the state of active crisis which results when:

1.   Internal strength and social support are lacking.
2.   The individual's problem remains unsolved.
3.   Tension and anxiety rise to an unbearable degree.

This Phase is usually accompanied by feelings of inadequacy and hopelessness, and, if prolonged to any real degree, becomes a state of 'learned helplessness' (Seligman, 1975).

9.3   The Crisis Plumage

Individuals, according to Hansell (1976), demonstrate certain characteristic regularities in behaviour when under crisis. Together

135

these characteristics create what Hansell calls the 'Crisis Plumage'. A synopsis of his ideas follows:

1. The individual shows a narrowed, fixed span of attention.
There is a failure to scan the whole environment adequately. This is apparent in attempts to solve the problem in traditional ways, and failure to seek out new solutions and new alternative sets of actions. Thoughts can be fixed on a particular theme, and it becomes difficult to get the client or person in crisis to change them or the subject. Usually such thoughts tend to be very ego-centric.

2. There is a tendency for the individual to 'loosen' and 'widen' affectional bonds.
When not in crisis, people usually engage a basic strategy for scanning the environment. This tends to become random only when their usual modus operandi begins to break down. We build up characteristic ways or patterns of structuring our lives and interacting with those around us. For those in crisis, according to Hansell, these habitual ways of behaving tend to break down and become more random.

This can be seen when the person-in-crisis moves away from those traditional ways of behaving, which relate and structure their lives. There may tend to be a decay in and a movement away from long established friendship patterns. In a similar way, people in crisis may begin to strike out from traditional family bonds, and 'pick up' new bonds and attachments. Hansell puts it this way: 'his social connection, his stable patterns of activity directed towards persons, groups, families and projects, show a characteristic decay of precision and pattern'.

3. The individual-in-distress experiences a profound loss of moorings to a clear vision of his identity.
This decay of the social connections mentioned by Hansell, leads concomitantly to a decay of identity. For most of us, we are able to summon a defining set of impressions of who we are, and of the nature of our capacities and skills. These tend to emanate, by and large, from our contact with 'significant others' in our environment. During crisis, however, the personal experience of identity becomes diffuse, vague and volatile.

To the person-in-crisis, it is almost as though the crisis belonged to someone else. This, of course, aids in the setting free from traditional connections, mentioned above. This loss of experience of identity may be dangerous, partly because it can mean that a new identity has to be forged, although that can be inherently growthful. The dangerous part of the experience is more because the decay in traditional bonds may lead to a widening set of contacts, which may become meaningful. If it appears to the person-in-distress that the new contacts 'have the answers', a kind of imprinting may occur, whereby bonding takes place with those who under non-crisis conditions may have been considered inappropriate targets of affection, adulation and the like.

If the crisis brings to the client feelings of inadequacy, associated with the belief that the situation is out of control, the helper has to be careful not to reinforce feelings of inadequacy. To do so may make those feelings within the client relatively permanent and difficult to change. Reinforcement may stem from the activities of insensitive helpers who want to 'do things for' the client in distress. This frequently derives from un-met needs within the helper - for example, to get a solution 'and then all will be happy'; because the emotional situation is too tough for the helper, or because the anxiety surrounding the crisis situation is unbearable for the helper. Ineffective helping of this kind can lead to a negation of self, diminution of self worth, depression and if severe enough, perhaps suicide, particularly if the anger phase mentioned earlier is turned inwards.

Because there is frequently a great degree of vulnerability associated with the client-in-crisis, he or she may tend to follow blindly those who promise a cure - whether this cure is offered by a shift into drugs, crime, religion or whatever.

4. The individual-in-distress quite regularly shows socially unsatisfactory performance of his roles.
According to Hansell, most behaviour during a crisis situation, including that related to the kinds of roles played, becomes more random, unstable and unpredictable. Protracted presentations of decayed role behaviour fragment social networks, which then deprive the person-in-crisis of the social support that Caplan believes important in stemming or ameliorating a crisis. Whilst the decay in traditional role behaviour provides the opportunity for the acquisition of new roles, these roles tend to be suggested by the environment within which the person-in-crisis finds himself. If he finds himself in a drug sub-culture or a radically different environment, he could well pick up attendant role behaviours. People in distress are amenable to manipulation for either better or worse.

5. There is an experience of an altered state of consciousness.
In line with previous comments, there is almost a random memory access mode, during which the individual in crisis will bring up unrelated segments of memory. There may well be a lack of a distinction between what was considered to be traditionally right and traditionally wrong. The person-in-crisis frequently perceives his world to be in a state of

flux. He seems neither to know who he is or where he is, at times. This brings about further alienation from traditional sources of support, family, friends and so on, who may find his thinking and his behaviour somewhat strange and more often than not somewhat bizarre.

6. The individual in distress experiences a drastically reduced ability to make decisions.

Decision-making involves steps of inventory, appraisal, decision, action, and review. These skills are markedly absent when an individual is in crisis. If Hansell is correct in assuming that thinking patterns become chaotic, then it is natural for the cognitive skills required to make decision to be impaired. Inventory-taking implies taking stock of the resources available to the person: strengths, weaknesses, skills, talents, community and family support. It involves an appraisal of what the problem is and being in a position to define it accurately, or to re-define (re-frame) it in a meaningful way. Then there is a need to make a decision and to accept responsibility for that decision. The outlining of the steps associated with making decisions, taking action, and following the decision through to the end-point, culminating in an evaluation of the progress made, is a kind of decision-making model similar to the model of the helping process outlined in an earlier chapter. Decision-making for the individual in distress may degenerate into emotional incoherent random behaviours which appear to have no real connectedness.

7. Individuals-in-distress send signals of distress.

These signals, according to Hansell, include posture, smell and sound, and function to alert group members to offer aid. Signals such as these are common to all mammals. Some of the immediate signs of emotional stress in humans are: sweating, hot flushes, tics, pallor, unusual speech, (for example, speech that is slurred, or much quicker than usual), poor sleeping habits, possible incontinence, and reduction in sexual activity.

9.4   Skills for Crisis Intervention

Okun (1976) reiterates that it is not the event that precipitates the crisis: the rape; alcoholic binge; suicide threats; acute bereavement; and so on that helpers work with, but the perceptions and the judgements held by the crisis victim. She asserts that helpers must rely greatly on their responsive communication skills both to get at the nature of the crisis and its stressful ramifications, and also communicate comfort, support and respect for the client. Common sense, calmness and the projection of self-confidence are very important. The ability to take some action may be very important. In crisis situations 'actions speak louder than words' particularly where there is a possibility of someone damaging themselves or another person.

Hoff (1978) believes that healthy crisis-coping can be facilitated by helpers by the utilisation of the following techniques:

1. listen actively and with concern
2. encourage the open expression of feelings
3. help the person gain an understanding of the crisis
4. help the individual gradually accept reality
5. help the person explore new ways of coping with problems
6. link the person to a social network (preferably a helpful one)
7. engage in decision counselling
8. reinforce the newly learned coping techniques and strategies and follow-up after the resolution of the crisis.

Decision-making counselling is cognitively orientated, and according to Hoff allows the upset person to put distorted thoughts, chaotic feelings, and disturbed behaviour into some kind of order. The person is encouraged to, inter alia:

a. search for boundaries of the problem
b. appraise the problem's meaning and how it can be mastered
c. make a decision about various solutions to the problem
d. test the chosen solutions in a clear-cut action plan.

The Mandala mapping procedure outlined in an earlier chapter could be usefully employed in crisis situations. Always remember that the articulation of the concern or problem makes it more controllable, in the sense that it is moving material into the Johari Window's 'area of free activity'.

9.5 Typical Coping Strategies

Hansell believes that individuals in crisis generate a crisis plumage which consists of characteristic ways of behaving and being. Helpers need to be aware that individuals tend to act or react in characteristic ways to anxiety-provoking situations. There may well be a tendency or proneness to 'fight or flight', to paralysis, to panic, or whatever. Generally speaking, individuals develop typical coping strategies as a way of handling crisis, and the anxiety that stems from crisis.

Coping strategies or defence mechanisms which people typically employ to reduce anxiety tend to have three basic characteristics. They are, first of all, used unconsciously - for the most part their use is out of the awareness of the person using them. They are, secondly, a means of coping with anxiety. Thirdly, they tend to distort reality. Many tranquilising drugs are prescribed and used throughout the world, and the belief is that they may temporarily prevent damage to the body by dampening down endocrine activity. The tranquilisers, per se, do not get rid of the underlying problem. They tend to mask it, and reduce its severity so that the body has time to repair itself.

In a similar way, it is legitimate for the individual to protect himself, by the use of coping strategies, against undue anxiety, but if these coping mechanisms are used constantly, and the individual continues to refuse to look squarely at the problem, then there may be pathological after-effects.

In the past, all defence mechanisms were thought to be pathological in character. The modern view is that they have a necessary function in giving time to the individual to think and work towards a resolution of the underlying problem. They may become pathological, however, if they are used to excess. Generally speaking, individuals employ characteristic ways of coping with anxiety, and therefore an individual will tend to use certain protective devices rather than others. The following list and brief description of some of the more common defence mechanisms or coping strategies is by no means exhaustive, and interested readers are referred to some of the basic texts in psychology.

Denial occurs when the individual flatly says 'No! It cannot be true...', or even more strongly - 'NO! NO! It is not true!' Denial comprises the first stage of the Kubler-Ross model of dying. This is when the dying patient, or the patient with an inoperable cancer is first told that they have only a certain period of time left to live, that their cancer is widespread, and so on. The NO! NO! protects the individual from the initial shock of the trauma of the revelation. It is a primitive response, and it really shuts off the anxiety by denying the existence of the noxious stimulus, on the premise that if it does not exist then it cannot do any harm. It is somewhat like the little child who hides her face, and because she does not see anything believes that she cannot be seen! Denial as a mechanism frequently works in conjuction with other defence mechanisms such as Repression.

Repression is a 'forgetting' of something that is unpleasant. The problem is of course that the forgetting is usually partial only, and the anxiety about the repressed event leaks through to cause the individual discomfort. It is as though the unpleasant event and its experience are pushed back into the recesses of the memory, and it becomes difficult to remember the painful events or situation. For example, the rape victim may never report the rape to the police or other authorities because having to recall, and retell the experience is a very painful process. The problem is that whilst the rape experience is repressed, it may continue to affect behaviour. For example, the rape victim may avoid contact with males, or develop ideas that sex is both dirty and painful.

A young teacher was accused of being too familiar with young girls in his care, by touching and fondling them. He was cautioned, but there were repeated allegations of misconduct, and he was asked to leave the school. The matter was 'hushed-up' and he was given the usual farewell rites. He went labouring for a while and was later approached by a boys' school and asked if he would consider teaching with them. This had been cleared with the authorities. He was a good teacher, and it was felt a waste that his talents within the classroom could not be utilised. The school made it clear to him that his background was known, but that there was a preparedness to give him a chance to re-enter teaching. He agreed. Within twelve months he was applying for positions in co-educational schools! He now argued that nothing had happened, and there was therefore no impediment to his being appointed to these schools. It is as though the whole painful series of events, together with the collusion from his original school, had been both denied and repressed.

Rationalisation is a very common form of defence mechanism. It happens when the individual gives excuses for his behaviour, attitudes and so on. The student who fails at school and blames his teachers, the system or an unfair examination for his failure is employing rationalisation. The student does this rather than look at himself as the source of his failure, or at least as a major contributor to it. Other examples might be the individual who has a meeting and therefore cannot be on time to meet his wife; the wife who develops a 'headache' in order to avoid love-making with her husband; the sadistic father who beats his children because 'it will do them good'. It should be added here that rationalisation is a relatively sophisticated and mature form of defence, in which we all engage, very obviously, from time to time!

Displacement is also a frequently used coping strategy, and occurs when the open expression of feelings, such as anger, hostility, love and concern, is threatening to the person wanting to express the feelings. What occurs is that the feelings are expressed to an inappropriate person or thing from which there is no possibility of 'retaliation'. The boss who is dominated by his wife, and who gets a verbal beating at breakfast, may smoulder all the way to work, and explode with angry feelings at his secretary, for no real reason. She becomes angry at being unfairly treated, and carries this into her home after work, where the kids on their return from school are castigated for minor misdemeanours. The eldest child passes it down the line to the youngest, who goes outside and kicks the dog. The dog then bays at the moon.

Reaction Formation is a subtle defence mechanism and is very difficult to detect. Reaction formation is the expression of one set of emotions which mask the opposite emotions. For example an expression of love and concern may mask hatred and hostility. For example, in the case study of Mike, his real feelings for his younger sister were of resentment and hostility, which he covered up by being too loving, too solicitous of her health and wellbeing. The possibility that reaction formation was operating can be noted by referring to the fact that he took his young sister on extremely long walks and had accidents which could have been fatal. Shakespeare was aware of this strategy when he believed that some people 'protest too much'.

Projection is the attribtuion to others of feelings, emotions, attitudes behaviour and so on that is the property of the person making the accusation. If an individual feels angry, he may argue that it is the other person who is angry. One of the writers working for a state welfare agency was summoned to the counter by the imperious ringing of the counter bell. A little old lady, wearing black, a shawl and a bonnet was at the counter. As soon as she saw that she was to be served, she banged on the counter with her umbrella saying 'don't you be angry with me - how dare you!' All before the officer concerned had uttered a word. The extreme form of projection can be seen in the psychiatric disorder called paranoia.

Regression is a retreat to an earlier form of behaviour, which at that time might have been deemed appropriate. But taking into account the present age and ostensible maturity of the individual is quite inappropriate. For example, a young child may sulk, and within bounds, it may be an appropriate response for her age. But sulking in a grown man is really quite inappropriate. Regressive behaviour sometimes takes place in a family where the youngest child is supplanted by the 'new baby'. As the 'new baby' grows and develops it receives praise for all its achievements: crawling, walking, talking etc. The supplanted child may resort to, for example, crawling, in order to get the attention and praise which has been given to the newest member of the family.

The next section of this chapter looks at the question of loneliness and how people cope with it. Loneliness represents a particular kind of emotional crisis for many people; it may accompany or underlie a more spectacular crisis. We need to be sensitive to the loneliness of others as an underlying factor or as a component in the everyday lives of our clients. We need to recognise that the experience of loneliness can deplete people's ability to cope with crises or just with life in general. Like many critical life experiences, loneliness can also be a powerful motivator and aid to personal growth.

9.6   Loneliness

Ritchie (1973) in a paper entitled 'Loneliness is a road to travel' explored the meaning of loneliness. He obtained the reactions of a group of young people to a loneliness encounter. A number in the group spoke of loneliness as an experience that filled them with dread, with self pity, with terrible loss. Most found the need for re-attachment to the world of things and people. For one person, the experience of loneliness was liberating.

The following are representative of some of the ways in which loneliness can be conceived

> Loneliness is being surrounded by people, but alone in your thoughts.

> Loneliness is no-one to share with; it's talk without communication; meeting without meaning. . .

> Loneliness is a feeling of unworthiness, of not being wanted; its the 'how are you' without expecting an answer, or which never gets a true one.

> Loneliness, Just Is. Aloneness is not loneliness. (Elvidge, 1973).

The hermit for instance - for him loneliness is the most creative element he has with which to shape his life. It is one of the conditions of his growth, his survival.

The deepest experiences a person can know are the lonely ones - the birth of a baby; the prolonged illness or death of a loved one; the creation of a poem; the painting of a picture, the composing of a symphony, completing a doctoral degree. Each of these in its own way touches upon the roots of loneliness. In each of these experiences we must go it alone. And grow because of it.

To see loneliness as a problem tied to anxiety and insecurity is to refuse to accept responsibility for so many things we must do alone. In so many things we are alone, our beliefs, our trusting, our birth and our dying. How we face loneliness is crucial. Face it one way, and life goes sour. Face it another way and life can be growthful. Individuals are caught up in the need to be apart from and yet to be a part of others, and it is the ability to handle both that leads to individual development. Loneliness is not just a matter of aloneness, it is more a recognition of the lack of deep and abiding connections with people which goes beyond the mere

143

interaction of one role to another for example, bank teller and customer. We meet, we say hello, we transact our business but we never encounter one another. Helping as conceived in this book sets up the possibility of an encounter between people, the helper and client, and the hope is that the encounter may well be a new experience for the client. It is the quality of the encounter that matters. If within the interview, helper and client encounter each other to some extent, then it is possible that the client may be prepared to encounter himself more deeply. Loneliness paradoxically occurs when we actually fail to encounter ourselves, for it is this failure that then sets us apart from others.

If we recognise the difference between aloneness and loneliness. If we, as helpers can be sensitive to the other's encounter with loneliness, and assist in the process of enabling the client to encounter himself more deeply, to use the process of the encounter in a creative way, then we may have truly been helpful. Being sensitive to the other's loneliness and all that that entails, requires an open-ness from us, where perhaps we really encounter our selves; it demands a listening to the other and to the self; it demands paying attention to the ideas, and the punctuation marks of silence and emotion, and searching for the meaning behind the meaning, both for ourself and for the client.

There are a number of strategies for coping with loneliness (see also Elvidge, 1973), some of which are outlined below. You can use these as aids to self-discovery. With care, they could be used with clients!

1. Identify the different kinds of loneliness you feel - write these on a sheet of paper, perhaps 10 responses to the question 'I feel lonely. . . when, if, because. . .' After you have done that, search for themes in the answers you have written, because we want you to go beyond a mere description of the situations etc. which make you feel lonely. After identifying the major themes, (if there are any) ask yourself the following question 'What does it mean to me if I feel lonely in this situation. . .' or 'How do I experience this feeling of loneliness?'.

If you can do this, or assist your clients to do this, then you are involved in the process of beginning the encounter with self. This will then help to identify those loneliness aspects which are creative and constructive and those which are destructive. On this basis, decisions can be made, strategies developed for enhancing the creative and minimising the destructive, or re-framing the destructive into becoming constructive.

2. The egocentrism of loneliness inhibits the possibility of sharing, and giving. Clients frequently employ mechanisms which cut them off from other people,although those mechanisms are ostensibly designed to attract others. For example, the young woman putting on too much perfume and too much make-up, designed to make her look attractive to males, in fact repels those whom she would like to attract, and attracts those she 'has' to repel. The person who talks too much or self-discloses inappropriately may appear, outwardly,to be open to others, but in fact others are embarrassed by the intensity of the disclosures and are repelled. It could be argued, of course, that the ostensible openness masks the fear of closeness and intimacy.

Part of the problem with egocentrism is that the individual tends to have really vague notions of the impact they are having on others. Work on video, on tape recorder, even in front of a full length mirror can be helpful in enabling the client to recognise the boundaries of their self. Similarly, a force-field analysis approach to the outlining of individual strengths and weaknesses could also be helpful.

3. Resource analysis must include feelings and emotions which add colour and depth to the personality. Many of our clients have 'monochrome' personalities which comes about largely through the inability to express themselves and their emotions. Use of music, literature, drama can be useful ways of enabling your client to feel the emotions as a starting point, and powerful ways of enabling safe expression of feelings. For example, expressing emotions by speaking only in numbers or nonsensical letters and getting people to identify the emotions expressed can be a useful way of facilitating people's approaching emotional expression more freely, and teaching clients a vocabulary of emotions and feelings. Not to share your feelings or your emotions - even anger - is also a form of deceit, and can lead people to experience us as untrustworthy or inconsistent.

4. Acknowledge that 'no man is an island' and that what it means to live, to be alive, is to be with others. It is interesting to note that it was the 'do your own thing' movement during the 1970's which formed the communes! Furthermore, who we are, is in part defined by who the others are. For example, Erikson (1963) talks about adolescents undergoing a crisis of identity in which some answer to the question 'Who am I' has to be made. He argues that young people are more interested in social intercourse than sexual intercourse, and that the meeting of male and female is the process of each defining for the other and for themselves the meaning of maleness and femaleness.

The helper may have to assist the client to make contact with others, and perhaps act as liaison in the initial stages. A tremendous amount of trust has to be built up between helper and client before this kind of move is contemplated.

145

Clients should be assisted to talk to people about how they feel, and about their loneliness if it really starts to get them down. As Elvidge points out, though, loneliness should not be covered up by intellectual chat, discussion or debate:

> 'You talk when you cease to be at peace with your thoughts; And when you can no longer dwell in the solitude of your heart, you live in your lips and sound is a diversion and a past-time. And in much of your talking, thinking is half murdered.
>
> For a thought is a bird of space, that in a cage of words may indeed unfold its wings but cannot fly.
>
> There are those among you who seek the talkative through fear of being alone.
>
> The silence of aloneness reveals to their eyes their naked selves and they would escape.
>
> And there are those who talk, and without knowledge or forethought reveal a truth which they themselves do not understand.
>
> And there are those who have truth within them, but they tell it not in words.
>
> In the bosom of such as these the spirit dwells in rhythmic silence.
>
> When you meet your friend on the road side or in the market place, let the spirit in you move your lips and direct your tongue.
>
> Let the voice within your voice speak to the ear of his ear.
>
> For the soul will keep the truth of your heart as the taste of wine is remembered.
>
> When the colour is forgotten and the vessel is no more.'
> (Elvidge, 1973)

The above extracts from 'Loneliness' by John Elvidge to a large extent encapsulate some of the meaning inherent in loneliness, including its potential for bitterness, as well as for growth and creativity. The fundamental skills learned as a helper should enable you to reach out to these people with care and sensitivity. Acceptance and a non-judgemental attitude are both very important. In a very real sense, the lonely person can be thought of as having a very restricted area of free activity as portrayed by the Johari Window. For trusting no-one, not even themselves, they are imprisoned within themselves and are unable to reach out to other people to make the kind of contact that ends loneliness.

9.7 Telephone Counselling

Recent research reported by Hornblow and Sloane (1979) indicated that life-line telephone counsellors were very effective in interpreting the feeling states of clients who had rung in for help. The helper perceptions of the effectiveness of the contact were also accurate. There is no doubt that telephone counselling can be effective. A great many of the contacts are from very lonely people, and the notions concerning clienthood apply equally to those who pick up the phone to make contact, as well as to those who come in to see a counsellor or helper. The demands on the helper are the same.

Obviously, you respond to the call with your name and the name of the agency, and then you ask how you may be of help. Simpson (1976) lists the procedures for managing crisis situations by phone :

(a) Establish rapport - 'I'm here - can I help ?'

(b) Elicit the problem - What is her problem ? Why has she called now ? What does she want from you ? Encourage her to talk.

(c) Clarify and paraphrase the problem.

(d) Evaluate the seriousness of the problem.

(e) Summarise the problem for your caller.

(f) Review tried and untried possible solutions.

(g) Agree upon a course of action for the client, for example, for her to be collected by taxi, for her to be visited, to be phoned hourly, to be accommodated somewhere, to be transported to a hospital casualty department, etc., or agree upon referral.

(h) Arrange a further contact or referral.

(i) Conclude with supportive counsel.

CAUTION
(a) Don't tackle serious crises - refer them to professionals.

(b) Don't attempt to use specialised counselling techniques .

(c) Don't think your telephone counsel has solved a crisis situation - at the most you have postponed one, so that effective intervention can begin.

(d) Don't undertake any lay or voluntary counselling unless you know about the various social and welfare services in your community, their facilities and their referral procedures.

Simpson goes on to set up criteria for evaluating the seriousness of the immediate situation, and his notes provide the basis for the following discussion.

9.8   Evaluating the Seriousness of the Immediate Situation
Calls range in seriousness from the bored person seeking company, diversion, or a chat, to the serious suicidee who has already overdosed before phoning. How do you tell how serious the problem is once it has been described or clarified? Evaluating seriousness is extremely difficult; there appear to be no simple texts on the topic, and once again we exemplify from our own practice.

On the basis of further training, careful reading, experience in phone counselling and sound supervision, we build up sets of criteria relating to particular problems, and use these to assess the seriousness of calls. Suicide threats are perhaps the most serious crisis calls, so we shall consider how one might evaluate such phone calls.

Epidemiology
When taking the call, it is useful to be able to answer the question as to whether this is the sort of person who seriously attempts suicide. In order to know that answer, you need to know the relevant epidemiology. So, for example, it would be helpful to know the proportion of males to females admitted to hospital per annum for suicide gestures; the method of choice for males and females in different age ranges; the age and sex distributions for successful suicides; and so on. Consultation with relevant statistical and descriptive material in your community is well advised.

Descriptive information of this kind, however, is not enough. Other reliable information on suicidal behaviour may be relevant. For example, what are the psychological backgrounds of those who commit suicide?

Barraclough (1974) has described a group of 100 suicides from his hospital:

(a) 93 were diagnosed mentally ill prior to having committed suicide

(b) 85 were clinical depressives and/or alcoholics

(c) 80 were seeing a doctor for their troubles

(d) 80 were receiving psychotropic drugs such as barbituric sedatives, antidepressants, phenothiazines, etc.

(e) 55 had given warnings of suicide

With respect to teenagers, there is a very high risk of suicidal gestures (but not successful suicide) amongst girls.

Schoolar (1973) writes as follows:

> Attempted suicide in adolescents is the culmination of a longstanding process of progressive isolation. There is no way out after previous attempts at resolution of problems have failed. It is a conscious rational decision from the perspective of the attempter who can see no other solution to the chronic problem of living.

Schoolar's (1973) claim that adolescents adopt suicidal gestures as a 'conscious rational decision' is supported by Lukianowicz, whose (1972) study of 100 young adult female patients in the Holywell Hospital in County Antrim, showed that such behaviour is largely successful in alleviating problems. Of his patients, approximately half were married. He followed up his research by contacting these women five years later, and found that only one had later committed suicide, while two had died of natural causes. Of the remaining 97, 75 had made positive gains, in 31 cases quite considerable gains; from their suicidal gestures, these women had gained changes in their husbands, who stopped playing around and became devoted; unwanted pregnancies were terminated, and the like.

Specificity of Plans
Clearly, epidemiological data takes us only so far. We also ask: 'How specific are her plans?' There are three important questions here:

(1) How lethal is the means of suicide she is talking about?

(2) Is the means immediately available to her?

149

(3) How specific are the plans she is giving you?

How often have you heard someone say that if something doesn't happen soon to change an unhappy situation, they will commit suicide? But careful interviewing reveals that they have only the most general (and often unrealistic) of plans, and have no lethal means immediately available. At the other end of the scale of seriousness is the man who calmly phones to say farewell to you, having first made a will, disposed of his belongings, bought a rifle which he has loaded and waiting by the phone before getting drunk.

There are several additional areas which we, as helpers, can refer to in assessing the seriousness of the suicidal call. They include:

A. The Precipitating Crisis
How serious is the immediate or chronic problem which has precipitated the suicide threat? If the precipitating crisis is great, for example, the spouse has unexpectedly died or run off, then you have to respond with maximum effort.

B. The Stress Symptoms
A number of gross symptoms clearly indicate seriousness. Further, depressed reactions such as despondency, despair, exhaustion, and loss of motivation for living, indicate high suicidal potential.

C. Personal Resources
What kind of state is your client in? Is she feeling completely helpless? You have to do something about this quickly. Does she have qualities, skills, attributes, etc. you can build on? Or are you having trouble calming her down, getting her to accept the possibility of hope, to accept advice on her confused ideas?

D. External Resources and Milieu
What resources does your client have available? Has she exhausted all available help and goodwill before phoning you in desperation? Are there various sources she will discuss with you that she has not used? For example, has she used parents, friends, doctor, psychiatrist, employer and so on, and been told that her problem is unalterable? Has her family concealed her problems? Does her husband refuse to allow her to go for help? Is she too proud to seek help, except anonymously over the phone? Is she aged, living alone without relatives, friends and neighbours to help?

Of the 100 suicides reported by Barraclough, 80 were going to the doctor at the time of their suicide. Nielsen and Videbach (1973) asked the question as to why this was the case. They believed that people who commit suicide go to a doctor often enough, but usually when they are past helping. An alternative view of this is of course, that they are past the kind of help that general practitioners usually can give! Perhaps, this reflects the fact that, often, general practitioners are inappropriate resources for people who really require a great deal of time and attention and for whom the prescription of tranquilisers and the like does not, ultimately, approach the real problem.

One of the authors engaged in a study of the use made by people of their general practitioner as a resource of help with social/psychological difficulties, (Gould, 1976). It was discovered, first of all, that the family doctor is often the only professional 'helper' with whom the client has ever had contact, and thus constitutes the only known resource or access point to formal helping systems in the community.

Secondly, the family doctor is often a known and trusted contact with whom the client feels safe and confident. As has been mentioned previously, it takes courage to be a client, and going to a known and trusted resource may make this process easier. Thirdly, the crisis, although social/psychological/emotional in nature, may make the client feel physically unwell - indeed, the client may in fact become physically unwell - and the doctor seems the appropriate contact. Responsibility rests, therefore, with the general practitioner to recognise the need for an onward referral. It is at this point that the system often breaks down, although not necessarily because the doctor is unable to make the correct assessment. It can often be the case that the client is unwilling to be referred on, or that appropriate helping agencies are not available, and so on. Many general practitioners do not have the time to spare to 'counsel' their patients, and very few, if any, have any training or expertise in counselling.

This reinforces the idea expressed earlier, therefore, that as helpers we have a responsibility to develop a network in the community with other professional helpers, health-care agencies, etc., so that we ourselves also become a known resource for referrals.

E. Other Factors
It is important to determine the health status of your client. Is she suffering from some terminal illness or chronic disease which involves pain, discomfort or debilitation? Many of those who commit suicide or attempt suicide have had frequent contact with hospitals and other health services. Ovenstone and Kreitman (1974) found that in broad terms those who commit suicide belong to one of two major groupings. One group lived stable, but precariously adjusted lives until the dislocation

occurred. The reaction was then a brief depressive period, sometimes associated with excessive drinking, and soon afterwards, suicide.

The other group were individuals with long term chronic personality problems, usually in association with chronic alcoholism, and who had a history of at least one parasuicidal episode. They tended to commit suicide in a setting of interpersonal chaos rarely associated with events that were independent of their own behaviour.

9.9   Suicide Intervention

People who threaten or attempt suicide as a way of coping with crisis usually lack more constructive ways of handling stress. The strategies mentioned previously in this book can be used by helpers when confronted by a suicidal client. Hoff (1978) believes that several techniques are particularly important for a helper to engage when working with a suicidal crisis:

1. relieve isolation
2. remove lethal weapons or means for commiting suicide
3. encourage alternative expressions of anger
4. avoid the client making a final decision of suicide during the crisis
5. re-establish social ties
6. relieve extreme anxiety and sleep loss - by medication initially.

Subsequently, there has to be the provision of quality 'after-care' following a suicide attempt. Unless this is provided, there is almost certainly going to be a further attempt, and of course, the chances of succeeding increase with the number of attempts made. Taylor (1979) reports on a '24 hour crisis intervention service' which he believes has markedly reduced suicidal recidivism, through the use of aggressive counselling, primarily psycho-analytic in orientation with suicidal individuals and their families. Taylor argues that whilst suicide is an individual act, in that the suicidal person makes the final decision, the suicidal decision arises out of the matrix of family interactions.

The suicidal person frequently makes the helper feel inadequate, lost, anxious and apprehensive that the client may terminate her life, in the helper's presence. Many helpers would then feel that in some way they were responsible for the suicide attempt, or that they had caused the death by not acting differently from the way that they did. It is extremely sad when another person takes his life, but the responsibility for that decision is the client's. It is very common, and in some degree seems natural, for a helper in such a situation to feel some guilt and remorse. However, helpers are not responsible for the actions of their clients, and every effort should be made to not view oneself, as helper, as having that kind of responsibility.

This chapter has been concerned with crisis and crisis counselling. Loneliness is frequently at the heart of many crises which result in suicide attempts. Workers should not believe that they are immune to crises. Self-conscious helpers recognise the value of professional supervision and of having colleagues they can depend upon in a crisis. Do not ever be afraid to be a client! Share your burdens, in much the same way you expect clients to share their worries and problems.

Loneliness can be painful, but it can also present the opportunity for growth, for a personal re-evaluation. Having 'time-out' can aid professional development particularly where 'alone-ness' may provide the possibility of reflecting on where you are at, as a worker, as a parent, as a person.

QUO VADIS?

Where do you go from here? This text does not pretend to provide you with all or even any of the answers to the problems that will confront you in your helping. If you want to progress in your development as a helping person, then you will need to read very widely, and practise your art, with a backing of theory from the social sciences, in a variety of settings, both with individuals and groups. You may care to take courses which concentrate on the development of helping skills. You may, indeed, become involved in a variety of groups which emphasise the development of self-awareness. Helping involves not only skills and personal awareness, however, it involves also the recognition that helping is a purposeful and informed intervention in the lives of others. Good intentions and warm feelings about people are not enough, and it is to be hoped that this text has provided you with an encounter with some of the theory from the social sciences which may illumine your helping activity.

Helping is a complex enterprise, not to be undertaken lightly, fraught with dangers for both the helper and the client. The major responsibility of the helper is to ensure that as far as possible, the relationship between the helper and the client is for better and not for worse. We have argued in this book for a growing self-consciousness within the helper, and for a continued commitment to helping. If you find yourself in any difficulty with a client, share your difficulty with a colleague or supervisor. Helping may be a real growth experience for the helper as well as the client.

APPENDIX A

Case Discussions

Case Discussion One - Freda.

Freda aged about 30 but looking a lot older came to see me about her son, whom she thought was backward. She explained to me that her husband had left her and had gone to live with another woman in another town. She described the other woman as the "local whore".

She had been left at home to look after her two children aged 9 and 10. The 10 year old was the one she was worried about and during the interview she complained bitterly about his behaviour. He will not do as he is told, 'he is quite naughty' and in fact has to be told repeatedly to do things. He seems to take great delight in being awkward, she said. The other child, also a boy, did not seem to warrant much attention. He caused her no trouble at all.

Freda was living with her brother and sister-in-law on a farm. In exchange for her keep, she did   odd jobs around the farm and got most of the meals for the family. Her sister-in-law was not altogether happy about Freda's presence on the farm. The sister-in-law was a very quick and efficient worker, and could do most jobs a great deal more quickly than Freda. She told Freda what she wanted, how each job was to be done and so on.

Freda's brother felt very sorry for Freda and used to "take-over" control of her children especially during the holidays. The ten year old child went to a "special school" and spent alternative holidays with the father (as did the other boy). The father had indicated that he would like custody of the two children. He however, had got his girlfriend pregnant; she has three children by her first marriage. Both the father and his girlfriend are seeking divorces and hope to marry, eventually.

Freda's elder son appeared to be "sub-normal"; thick lips, a funny voice and funny ears and seemed to cock his head on one side most of the time. I

155

had an opportunity to observe this family at a meal time. Freda was continually 'on her elder son's back', telling him to eat nicely and not to gobble his food down. "Mummy likes nice boys, who eat their food up properly"; "I've told you once, and I'll not tell you again do not eat your peas with your knife" and so it went on for most of the meal. The boy appeared not to take notice and it was at this stage that Freda's brother would chip in and say "I'll belt you if you do that again".

Freda continually apologised for the meal which she reckoned was not well cooked. She said this more than once!

Questions for discussion

1. What, if anything is "wrong" with this family?

2. Do you think that Freda needs help? If you do, what kind of help?

3. How would you handle the elder son?

4. What is the sister-in-law doing for and to Freda?

5. What are they doing for and to themselves?

6. What else is happening in this family?

7. Freda has talked about leaving home and working in the nearest town. Is this a good idea?

Additional Information: If you were told that Freda had spent some time in a psychiatric (mental) hospital would this change any of your ideas?

To understand and perhaps begin to 'solve' this problem what further information do you think you would need?

Do you think these children will end up in a psychiatric hospital, if things do not change, or do you think they may become delinquent and end up in a detention centre or jail?

Can anything be done for this family?

Remember Freda came for help!

Case Discussion Two - Tony

Tony was 9 years old when he first came to the notice of the police. He was suspected of having been involved with a group of other boys in burning down the state primary school. He came under notice several more times for theft of goods, mainly from unlocked cars, but as he was 'under-age' he did not appear in the children's court for these offences. However, he did appear in court two years ago, aged 13 for a whole long line of stealing offences. He was made a state ward and placed in a foster home. Within 6 months of being made a state ward he had been placed in two foster homes, through no fault of his own. In one of the placements, the foster parents became quite ill and could not care for him. In the other placement, the family were suddenly transferred to another centre, and as it was unreasonable to shift Tony too far away from his natural home, he was placed with another local family. He stayed with them for about 8 months and this broke down because of Tony's alleged lying. Money had gone missing and he had been accused of taking it. There was a continuing deterioration in relationships between Tony and his foster parents. This culminated in their asking for him to be removed.

There was an acute shortage of good foster homes, so it was decided (expediently) to place Tony back in his own home on a trial basis under the supervision of a very experienced welfare officer. Tony stayed out of trouble for approximately another 12 months, and then this officer was transferred to another district. Tony again appeared in court on a number of charges; breaking and entering; stealing; car conversion. Most of the offences were 'solo efforts', and the ill-gotten gains were usually secreted under his bed, or in his wardrobe.

Tony was the middle child of five. Mother went to work more or less for 'social' reasons. She had little patience with Tony, and seemed glad when he was taken away from home. She was not prepared to accept responsibility for him in any shape or form. The house was mainly tidy, but officers visiting the house used to complain about the dogs (5) and the cats (3) (and goldfish!) that seemed to be everywhere. The house was located in a beach-side suburb. Father worked extremely long hours in his own business as a plumber, and could not offer any explanation for Tony's behaviour. Tony disliked his mother intensely, and tried to get 'alongside' dad. Tony's father also commented that he could not really see anything wrong with Tony's behaviour "After-all boys will be boys! You ought to have seen what I got up to when I was a boy!" He was too busy to have much time for Tony.

Relationships between Tony and his brothers and sisters (two of each) appeared to be good. At school, Tony had difficulty, and occasionally would take a day off. He was a 'bit of a loner' according to his teacher.

She wondered why he got into so much trouble, he was such a nice lad, with a rosy, cherubic face!

As a result of the last court appearance, Tony was placed in a long term institution, where he stayed for 30 months. He was described as a model 'inmate'. His parents rarely visited him, the institution was in another State. He behaved himself when on leave at home. He made progress in all school subjects whilst in the institution. He was fifteen, nearly sixteen when he was released from the institution. The institution prided itself on the quality of its caring, and there is no doubt that Tony made considerable progress.

Questions for discussion

1. What kind of prognosis would you suggest for Tony? What are your reasons for saying this?

2. What might be some of Tony's needs, and how might they be met upon his release?

3. What are some of the themes which seem to emerge from Tony's history?

4. What further knowledge or information do you think it might be helpful to know, if you were the welfare worker appointed to supervise Tony upon his release?

5. What might be important tasks for the worker to undertake prior to and subsequent upon Tony's discharge?

Case Discussion Three - Hazel

Hazel lived in a government subsidised house in a suburb comprised mainly of low-income housing. Her husband had committed suicide the previous year. She was receiving financial and counselling assistance from the social welfare department. Hazel has two young children to support (aged 3 and 18 months).

A new social worker took over the case and discovered that Hazel had the habit of ringing up the department last thing on a Friday afternoon, demanding money for the weekend. She was in the habit of saying there was no food in the house, and that the children were hungry. Previous social workers had recognised this need and had gone dutifully out of their way to ensure that she was given a grant that would see her get through the weekend. They used to travel the 50kms there and back to give her the money. The previous social workers had remonstrated with her about the need to budget her resources in a more adequate and appropriate way.

Hazel had no car and no telephone. She used to ring from her neighbours house. As the public transport system in this suburb was practically non-existent, Hazel used to hire taxis to get her into the local shopping area (about 3 kms from her home).

Questions for discussion

1. In what way were the previous workers' actions helpful?

2. In what way were the previous workers' actions not helpful?

3. How would you consider helping Hazel?

4. What additional knowledge or information would be helpful to you in your assistance to Hazel?

Additional information: Would you want to handle this case any differently if you discovered that Hazel's husband committed suicide?

Appendix B **A Model of the Communication Process**   Weaver — 1967

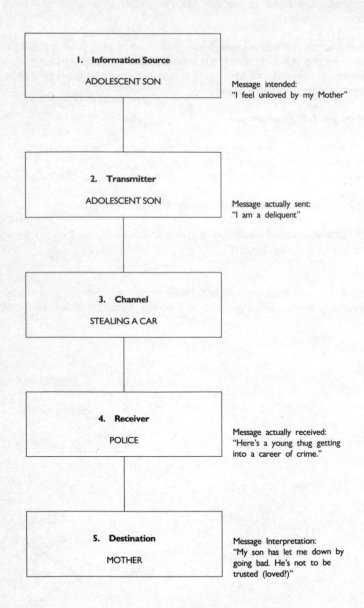

1. **Information Source**

   ADOLESCENT SON

   Message intended:
   "I feel unloved by my Mother"

2. **Transmitter**

   ADOLESCENT SON

   Message actually sent:
   "I am a deliquent"

3. **Channel**

   STEALING A CAR

4. **Receiver**

   POLICE

   Message actually received:
   "Here's a young thug getting
   into a career of crime."

5. **Destination**

   MOTHER

   Message Interpretation:
   "My son has let me down by
   going bad. He's not to be
   trusted (loved?)"

BIBLIOGRAPHY

Adams, J., Hayes, J., and Hopson, R. (1976) **Transition:**
Understanding and Managing Personal Change,
London, Martin Robertson

Asch, S.A. (1952) **Social Psychology,** Englewood Cliffs, Prentice-Hall

Barraclough, B. (1974) '100 cases of suicide : clinical aspects',
Brit. J. Psychiat., 125

Barrett-Lennard, G.T. (1962) 'Dimensions of therapist response
as causal factors in therapeutic change', **Psychological**
Monographs General and Applied, 76, 43, 1-33

Becker, H.S. (1963) **Outsiders,** New York, Free Press

Berenson, B.C. and Mitchell, K.M. (1974) **Confrontation For Better Or**
For Worse, Amherst, Mass., Human Resource Development Press

Berry, J.W. (1972) 'Radical Cultural Relativism' in Berry, J.W. and
Dasen P.R. (1974) **Culture and Cognition : Readings in Cross**
Culture Psychology,

Biestek, F.P. (1934, 1957) **The Casework Relationship,** Chicago,
Illinois, Loyola University Press

Bordin, E.S. (1968) **Psychological Counselling (2nd Edition),**
Englewood Cliffs, Prentice-Hall

Bowlby, J. (1960) 'Separation Anxiety', **International Journal of**
Psychiatry, 41 (89-113)

Brammer, L.M. and Shostrom, E.C. (1977) **Therapeutic Psychology**
(3rd Edition), Englewood Cliffs, Prentice-Hall

Caplan, G. (1964) **Principles of Preventive Psychiatry**
New York, Basic Books

Carkhuff, R.R. (1969) **Helping and Human Relations : Volume 1
- Selection and Training,** New York, Holt, Rinehart and
Winston

Carkhuff, R.R. and Berenson, B.G. (1967) **Beyond Counselling and
Therapy,** New York, Holt, Rinehart and Winston

Colin, J. (1974) **Never Had It So Good,** Victor Gollancz

Cozby, P.C. (1973) 'Self-Disclosure : A Literature Review',
Psychological Bulletin, 79, 73-91

Cumming, J. and Cumming, E. (1962) **Ego and Milieu : theory and
practice of environmental therapy,** New York, Atherton Press

Egan, G. (1975) **The Skilled Helper : A Model for Systematic
Helping and Interpersonal Relating,** Monterey, California,
Brooks/Cole

Egan, G. (1976) **Interpersonal Living : A Skills/Contract Approach
to Human Relations Training in Groups,** Monterey, California,
Brooks/Cole

Ellis, A. (1973) **Humanistic Psychotherapy : The Rational-Emotive
Approach,** New York, Julian Press

Elvidge, J. (1973) 'Loneliness', **NZ Social Worker,** 8, 4

Epstein, R. and Koromita, S.S. (1966) 'Prejudice among Negro children
as related to parental ethnocentrism and punitiveness', **Journal
of Personal Social Psychology,** 4

Erikson, E.H. (1963) **Childhood and Society (2nd edition),**
New York, Norton

Festinger, L. (1957) **A Theory of Cognitive Dissonance,** Evanston,
Illinois, Rowe Peterson

Fischer, J. (1973) **Interpersonal Helping,** Springfield, Ill.,
Charles Thomas

Fischer, J. (1978) **Effective Casework Practice : An Eclectic Approach,**

New York, McGraw-Hill

Fix, A.J., and Haffke, E.A. (1976) **Basic Psychological Therapies: Comparative Effectiveness,** New York, Human Sciences Press

Gilliland, B.E. and Davis, R.E. (1974-83) **Focus on client growth in systematic counselling : Stages in the systematic counselling model,** Memphis State University, Tennessee, Department of Counselling and Personnel Services, unpublished graduate circular handout distributed in courses on theories and techniques of counselling

Glasser, W. (1965) **Reality Therapy,** New York, Harper and Row

Good, T.L. and Brophy, J.E. (1973) **Looking in Classrooms,** New York, Harper and Row

Gould, S.J. (1976) 'The general practice and social work : report on a trial', **Medical Journal of Australia, 1**

Haley, J. (1968) 'Communication, Family and Marriage', in Jackson, D.D. **Human Communication Volumes 1 and 2,** Palo Alto, California, Science and Behaviour Books

Halmos, P. (1965) **The Faith of the Counsellors,** London, Constable

Hamachek, D.E. (1978) **Encounters with the Self** (2nd Edition), New York, Holt, Rinehart and Winston

Hansell, N. (1976) **The Person in Distress: On the Bio-social Dynamics of Adaptation,** New York, Human Sciences Press

Hoff, L.E. (1978) **People in Crisis: Understanding and Helping,** Calif., Addison-Wesley Publishing

Holmes, T.H., and Rahe, R.H. (1967) 'The social readjustment rating scale', **Journal of Psychosomatic Research,** 11, 213-218

Hornblow, A. (1980) 'The Study of Empathy', **NZ Psychologist,** 8, 19-28

Hornblow, A. and Sloane, H. (1979) 'An evaluation of the effectiveness of Life-line', Unpublished paper presented at the Jubilee Conference, NZ Psychological Society, Wellington.

Ivey, A. (1971) **Micro Counselling : Innovations in Interview Training,**

Springfield, Illinois, Charles Thomas

Ivey, A. and Authier, J. (1978) **Micro Counselling : Innovations in Interviewing, Counselling, Psychotherapy and Psychoeducation, (2nd Edition)**, Springfield, Illinois, Charles Thomas

Jackson, D.D. (1968) **Communication, Family and Marriage, Volumes 1 and 2**, Palo Alto, Science and Behaviour Books

Jourard, S.M. (1971) **Self-disclosure : An Experimental Analysis of the Transparent Self** , New York, Wiley Inter-Science

Kahneman, D. (1973) **Attention and Effort**, Englewood Cliffs, Prentice-Hall

Kastenbaum, R. (1975) 'Is death a life crisis? On the confrontation with death in theory and practice', in Datan, N. and Ginsberg, L.H.(eds) **Life-Span Developmental Psychology: Normative Life Crises**, New York, Academic Press

Keith-Lucas, A. (date unknown) 'The Art and Science of Helping', Case Conference

Krause, A.H. (1976) 'Who is the You Nobody Knows?', **Personnel and Guidance Journal**, April

Kubler-Ross, E. (1969) **On Death and Dying**, New York, Macmillan

Laing, R.D. (1970) **Knots**, London, Tavistock

Lewin, K. (1935) **Conflict Theory : A Dynamic Theory of Personality**, New York, McGraw-Hill

Lindemann, E. (1944) 'Symptomatology and management of acute grief', **American Journal of Psychiatry**

Loughary, J. and Ripley, T.M. (1979) **Helping Others Help Themselves**, New York, McGraw-Hill

Luft, J. (1969) **Of Human Interaction**, Palo Alto, California, National Press Books

Lukianowicz, N., (1972) 'Suicidal behaviour : An attempt to modify the environment', **Brit. J. Psychiat.**, 123

Lyman, S.M. and Scott, M.B. (1970) **The Sociology of the Absurd,**
New York, Appleton-Century-Crofts

McCluskey, H.Y. (1970) 'An Approach to a Differential Psychology
of the Adult Potential' in Grabowski, S.M. (ed) **Adult
Learning and Instruction,** Syracuse,New York, E.R.I.C.
Clearinghouse on Adult Education

MacLean, D. (1980) 'When is a counsellor a counsellor? Some
thoughts on the shift from 'becoming' a counsellor to
'being' a counsellor', **The Counsellor,** 3, 1, 23-30

MacLean, D. (1980a) **An Introduction to the Helping Process -
Introductory Notes on Counselling,** Hamilton, NZ.
Centre For Continuing Education, University of Waikato

Maslow, A.H. (1968) **Toward a Psychology of Being (2nd edition),**
New York, Van Nostrand

Mauksch, H.O. (1975) 'The organisational context of dying' in
Kubler-Ross, E. **Death : The Final Stage of Growth,**
Englewood Cliffs, Prentice-Hall, Spectrum

Mayeroff, M. (1971) **On Caring,** New York, Harper and Row

Mead, G.H. (1934) **Mind, Self and Society,** Chicago, University
of Chicago Press

Nielsen, J. and Videbach, T. (1973) 'Suicide frequency before
and after introduction to community psychiatry in a
Danish island', **Brit. J. Psychiat.,** 123

Okun, B.F. (1976) **Effective Helping, Interviewing and
Counselling Techniques,** North Scituate, Mass.,
Duxbury Press

Ovenstone, I.M.K. and Kreitman, N. 1974 'Two syndromes of
suicide', **Brit. J. Psychiat.,** 124

Pease, A. (1981) **Body Language,** North Sydney, Camel Publishing

Postle, D. (1980) **Catastrophe Theory,** Glasgow, Fontana Paperbacks

Ritchie, J.E. (1973) 'Loneliness... is a road to travel
and beyond', **NZ Social Worker,** 8, 4

Rogers, C.R. (1951) **Client-Centred Therapy,** Boston, Houghton-Mifflin

Rogers, C.R. (ed) (1967) **The Therapeutic Relationship And Its Impact,** Madison, University of Wisconsin Press

Schoolar, J.C. (ed) (1973) **Current Issues in Adolescent Psychiatry,** New York, Bruner-Mazel

Seligman, M.E.P. (1975) **Helplessness,** Reading, W.H. Freeman

Sherif, M. (1936) **The Psychology of Social Norms,** New York, Harper

Simpson, D.W. (1976) **Helping Others,** Waikato University, Hamilton, New Zealand, Centre for Continuing Education

Stewart, N.R., Winborn, B.B., Johnson, R.G., Burks, Jr., H.M., and Engeltes, J.R. (1978) **Systematic Counselling,** Englewood Cliffs, Prentice-Hall

Truax, C.B., and Carkhuff, R.R. (1967) **Toward Effective Counselling and Psychotherapy,** Chicago, Aldine

Volkman, R. and Cressey, D.R. (1963) 'Differential association and the rehabilitation of drug addicts', **American Journal of Sociology,** 69, 2

Watzlawick, P., Beavin, J.H., and Jackson, D.D. (1967) **Pragmatics of Human Communication : A Study of Interactional Patterns, Pathologies and Paradoxes,** New York, Norton

Watzlawick, P., Weakland, J.H.,and Fisch, R. (1974) **Change : Principles of Problem Formation and Problem Resolution,** New York, Norton

Weaver, W. (1967) **Science and Imagination, Selected Papers,** New York, Basic Books

Woolf, V. 'To The Lighthouse', extract in Cooper, J. (1981) **Violets and Vinegar,** Oxford

Yeoman, L.A. (1984) **Empathic Understanding : Mythical or Mystical,** Unpublished Master's Thesis, University of Waikato, Hamilton, New Zealand

INDEX

Index

Index